GROWING HOME
Stories of Ethnic Gardening

Susan Davis Price

Photography by John Gregor/ColdSnap Photography

University of Minnesota Press
Minneapolis • London

The University of Minnesota Press gratefully acknowledges assistance provided for the publication of this volume by the John K. and Elsie Lampert Fesler Fund.

Jacket and text design by Lois Stanfield, LightSource Images, Minneapolis

Published by the University of Minnesota Press
111 Third Avenue South, Suite 290
Minneapolis, MN 55401-2520
http://www.upress.umn.edu

Library of Congress Cataloging-in-Publication Data
Price, Susan Davis.
    Growing home : stories of ethnic gardening / Susan Davis
  Price : photography by John Gregor/ColdSnap Photography.
      p.   cm.
    ISBN 0-8166-3305-3 (hardcover). — ISBN 0-8166-3306-1 (pbk.)
    1. Gardening—Minnesota Anecdotes. 2. Gardeners—Minnesota
Anecdotes. 3. Gardening—Philosophy.   I. Title.
SB455.P75 2000
635′.09776—dc21   99-38320

Printed in China by HK Scanner Arts Int'l Ltd

The University of Minnesota is an equal-opportunity educator and employer.

11 10 09 08 07 06 05 04 03 02 01 00   10 9 8 7 6 5 4 3 2 1

CONTENTS

ACKNOWLEDGMENTS

In researching and writing a book, the author must lean
heavily on friends and colleagues for advice and support.
I have been fortunate to work with generous, competent people
throughout this project. I am grateful first to Todd Orjala,
editor at the University of Minnesota Press, who suggested
this topic and cheered me on. My good friend Rick Rykken
read the entire manuscript and made his usual intelligent
comments. John Gregor took the wonderful photographs,
capturing the essence of each garden. As always, my family
listened with empathy to the joys and trials of writing.

Especially, I am grateful to the resourceful, open-hearted
gardeners who invited me into their homes. They fed me,
sent me home with fresh produce, told me about their
gardens, and trusted me with the stories of their lives.
To them I dedicate this book.

INTRODUCTION

Humans are migratory animals, trooping across the globe in search of food, land, work, adventure, social equality, and peace. What is true of people generally is especially true of Americans, arriving from foreign shores and then traveling westward. Devastation in other countries, from famine to overpopulation, has sent wave after wave of immigrants to try their luck in the United States. For many, Minnesota has been the destination.

In the Twin Cities, we are especially aware of some of our newer groups, the ones who come in large numbers. The 1970s and 1980s saw immigrants from Asia, and Africa was the home continent for many who arrived in the 1990s. But immigrants are still coming from Finland and Greece, Switzerland and Italy. They are not settling just in Minneapolis and St. Paul, but in Anoka, Coon Rapids, Duluth, Pipestone, and Madelia. Though

many come because of political upheaval or repression, others come for education or love.

As they travel, people carry their plants, brought purposefully in trunks and bags, or unwittingly on boots and clinging to mittens. In the late 1600s, the Ojibwe, pushed west to Minnesota by white settlement, brought seeds of corn, pumpkins, beans, squash, and potatoes. Two hundred years later, Norwegians came with beet and cabbage seeds, apple tree scions, and rhubarb roots. As the Hmong arrived in the 1970s and 1980s, they brought seeds of various mustards, melons, and squash, and cuttings of their medicinal plants. "We were afraid we couldn't find these plants here," one of the Hmong gardeners told me, echoing what many have felt leaving their homelands.

For plants are of great importance in most cultures. In much of the world, gardening is not simply

an agreeable pursuit, a hobby like working crossword puzzles. Rather, it is an essential: no garden, no food. Even in countries like England, where food can be obtained easily from the market, gardening is integral to community life.

Though some Americans have lost that connection to the earth, we preserve it in our language. We speak of "putting down roots," "cultivating" friendships, "plowing" ahead, "planting" an idea. We admire someone who is "down-to-earth" or "rooted," and we're pleased when our friends "blossom," even if they are "late bloomers."

But for most of the people I met, gardening was not simply a metaphor. Time and again I heard, "Everyone in my country gardens," followed by a detailed description of the vivid landscapes at home. No wonder, then, that many new arrivals try to reproduce at least part of their home grounds after settling in Minnesota. Even I, moving here from Louisiana, insisted on planting azaleas, as plentiful in the South as lilacs are in Minnesota. At the time, I had little from which to select because few had been hybridized for this cold climate. So unusual were my bright shrubs that people stopped to stare and inquire when they were in bloom. If I felt a sense of dislocation in simply moving several states north, how much more displaced must people from Laos and Guatemala feel?

In planning this book, I was looking for three things: gardeners in all corners of the state, gardeners from as many countries and backgrounds as possible, and people who are passionate about their avocation. Happily, I found diversity more genuine than any arbitrary categories could define. I met flower specialists as well as fruit and vegetable growers. They grew plants in circles, in long rows, in pots, in thickets. There were gardeners in their thirties and one ninety-five-year-old. Some were impressive because they could get buckets of produce from a small space, and others because of the enormous gardens they tended.

The range of plants, including many I had never seen, was eye-opening. Alida Olson, who lives near Glenwood, grows ground-cherries and an eight-foot-tall flower called prince's-feather *(Polygonum orientale)*. Joe Braeu in Duluth raises heaths and heathers. Bokson Pyunn cultivates the crown daisy flower *(Crown coronarium)* for her stir-fry dishes, while Tae Young Lee grows wild sesame *(Perilla frutescens)* and *toduk (Codonopsis pilosula)*. I saw Cuban oregano, Sicilian basil, Turkish peppers, Chinese eggplant, Korean zucchini, French cucumbers, and Greek tomatoes.

I discovered that many groups cultivate or forage for plants that mainstream Americans work hard to eradicate from their lawns and gardens. With only a few seasonings, dandelions, as well as purslane and lamb's-quarters, stinging nettle and amaranth, become tasty and healthful dishes. Nearly half of the gardeners grow or collect plants for their medicinal value. Seeing this diversity made me realize what a paltry few hundred plants are commonly cultivated in American yards.

Despite their differences, the gardeners profiled here have a number of striking similarities. All are keenly aware of the nutritional benefits of the produce they grow, and contrast the quality of their homegrown vegetables to those found at market. Very few use chemicals. Though a handful apply commercial fertilizer, all work on improving the soil with manure, leaves, and compost. Many mentioned strong concerns about the use of pesticides and herbicides and their effects on people.

As a group, these gardeners are impressively healthy. Though several are in their eighties and nineties, they are still living independently, gardening vigorously, and enjoying life. The case of the Koreans living at Cedar-Riverside apartments is telling. There, thirty-three Korean elders, aged sixty to ninety, live and garden. The social worker helping them brought a caseworker from the Hennepin County Assisted-Living Program to evaluate the aging residents. Perhaps, she thought, they could become clients of Assisted-Living. After going through the evaluation process, the caseworker reached this conclusion: none of the gardeners qualify because they're all too healthy.

The gardeners' most striking similarity, though, is their frequent and impassioned emphasis on the psychological and spiritual benefits of working the soil. When the first person I interviewed mentioned the peace she found among her herbs and flowers, I was fascinated. The second gardener told me that working with his plants gave him "balance" and a sense of perspective about life. Then I spoke with Chue Yang, who said that going to her garden made her feel alive again after a long day at the office. One of the last people I met said that gardening is a spiritual undertaking.

I came to expect that at some point in our interview, people would share the deep satisfactions of caring for plants. These feelings were present regardless of the culture or country from which they came. Indeed, though the specific ways people plant and harvest are quite varied, the ways they feel about what they do are similar. Perhaps we're hardwired to till and plant. Not so long ago in America, to garden was to survive, and it still is today in many other countries. Surely there must be positive connections in the brain for such an

essential activity. A corollary: do we suffer physically and psychologically when we lose that connection with the earth?

This book, then, is the story of thirty-one different Minnesota gardens. Some of the gardeners have been in the state for several months; others can trace their lineage back for generations. Yet all are growing some of their heritage in growing their gardens.

The book is not meant to be a horticultural "how-to," though a great deal of gardening information—plant names and planting styles—is embedded in each story. Instead I've looked at why people garden. The book has five major divisions: the beauty, the joy, the taste, the lessons, and the peace of home. In reality, my assignment of each gardener to one of these sections was an arbitrary choice. Many of them grow for all these reasons. Certainly, some of the folks growing vegetables as staples do so as well for the joy or peace it brings them. Likewise, those who grow for the beauty are also finding lessons in their work.

Finding these gardeners turned out to be much harder than I had assumed. The general requests I made via the Internet and electronic lists were fairly unproductive. Instead, most of the names came to me one at a time. The mother-in-law of a friend had seen a short feature on her local cable station in Luverne about a Laotian gardener in Pipestone. When I gave a talk in Ely on garden history, someone in the audience told me of the wonderful garden of Angie Smith, originally from Slovenia. I read an article about a fellow from Germany living in Duluth. A neighbor said there was an incredible Norwegian lady near her cabin.

For every lead that worked, three headed nowhere. A Lebanese gardener had grown too old. Someone from Russia had lost her access to the community plot. Another had left the state.

Often I would have a name, a country of origin, and a telephone number. I would call and try to explain my project, then ask for an interview. What must my respondents have felt, getting a call from a stranger who wanted to talk to them about their gardens? Yet they were unfailingly gracious once they understood my request. "Of course, come on over, but the garden doesn't look so good—yet," or "anymore," or "this summer."

They opened their homes and gardens to me, fed me, sent me home with fresh produce. I had a sense of eating my way around the state, and, because of the varied cuisine, eating my way around the globe. Homegrown leeks wrapped in hand-rolled phyllo pastry are in a class above the best restaurant fare. Tamales made fresh and steamed in just-cut corn leaves, served with homemade salsa, taste nothing like the tamales I was used to.

Meeting these gardeners inspired me, giving me hope for the future. I felt that I had been introduced to a vast, invisible network of people living full, well-integrated lives. They reminded me that, even in the midst of a culture nourished on fast foods and hurried entertainments, it is still possible to live in concord with the rhythms of the earth.

GARDENING FOR BEAUTY

Judy Oakes Wehrwein

AN ENGLISH COTTAGE GARDEN

eave to others the scientific study of gardening—soil testing, Latin names, and the like. Judy Oakes Wehrwein prefers the hands-on method. "I quite appreciate that others like to talk earnestly about the merits of various cultivars," she said in her gentle British accent. "But that's not me. I'll see a flower I like and put it in my own garden, but then completely forget its name."

Nor does Judy plot her borders on paper or keep a record of what's planted. "No," she laughed, "I wait to see what comes up in the spring, because there are always surprises. You'll think something should be in one spot and then, oh dear, something's happened to it."

No matter. Judy's St. Paul garden looks wonderful in all seasons. Spring bulbs and early-season beauties like bergenia and Siberian iris are followed by peonies and baptisia. In high summer, astilbes, delphiniums, dictimus, and roses

add the pastel colors she loves. Clematis cascade over the wooden fence and climb the front of the house. Autumn brings coneflowers, boltonia, phlox, hardy asters, and chelone. Even in winter the yard is eye-catching, with its perfectly clipped, snow-draped yews and lit-up greenhouse filled with the yellows of forced daffodils, the reds of geraniums and amaryllis, and the blues of streptocarpus. In Judy's hands, the glory of English gardening is made manifest.

Perhaps the hands-on method works well for Judy because she comes from such a strong gardening tradition. "Everybody in England had some kind of garden," she observed. "You just didn't not garden. Of course, some people were more effective than others, but everybody had something."

In a culture like that, much is learned by osmosis. "My mother had wonderful gardens," she said,

Judy, age twelve, and her brother, Roger, in their mother's garden in Hatch End, Middlesex, England. Photograph courtesy of Judy Wehrwein.

The Wehrweins' first Minnesota home, a suburban colonial, never felt like home. They moved to this Cape Cod house in St. Paul, and after she added her English borders, Judy knew that this was "home."

"first in suburban London, where I grew up, and then in Devonshire. It was part of the ritual when company came to go 'round the garden.' And you really went round the garden. I kind of liked that. It would be slightly gossipy as you walked. You'd catch up on the relatives and neighbors. But, of course, you also talked about how the plants were doing. I grew up with that ritual."

Wehrwein may not delve into the science of horticulture, but she is an astute observer. "I'm a visual person," she explained. "I get ideas at garden centers and on tours, and, of course, from being in my mother's gardens. And I like to just go out and stand and stare at the garden.

You learn not to set plants out in a line like soldiers and how to chose interesting textures. You see that it's nice to contrast a spiky plant with a soft, mounded one."

She's learned a great deal through years of working with the plants and soil. "Wherever I've been, I've had a garden," she said. "The early ones, when we had small children, were not as extensive as this, but they were important to me."

Judy met her American husband in London after World War II when they both worked at the U.S. Embassy. They spent a year in Denmark, then moved to the United States in 1951, coming to Minnesota in the late 1960s and ending up in St. Paul in 1978. This last garden has received the most attention from Judy. When the Wehrweins arrived, there were few flowers on their property; today there is only a bit of lawn left.

Now that she's retired, Judy can work outside long hours every day. But even when she held a full-time job, Judy went to the garden each evening until dark, and worked for six or seven hours on weekends. "Often we wouldn't eat dinner until eight o'clock," she chuckled. "Hard work, hard work, hard work, but I just love doing it. I've always liked physical labor. Even when I'm utterly miserable with the bugs and the heat and I look ghastly with muddy knees and dripping hair, I'm very happy."

Happy, no doubt, but not entirely satisfied. "Not really," she insisted. "No. It's never quite right. I can always think, oh dear, this has died

Wehrwein's front-yard garden is a success, not only for its colorful plants, but because of the interesting fence that defines the area. Philippe Gallandat had a hand in its design.

and that is flopping over. So, there will be a stretch here and I'll say to myself, yes, that looks really nice, or that over there looks good today. But I'd like it all to look wonderful at the same time. I do console myself to a certain extent that all those beautiful pictures you see in magazines have been taken at the optimum moment."

However, the garden's flaws are not so obvious to her neighbors, who go out of their way to stroll by. "They often thank me for adding to their enjoyment," she said. Even neighborhood children have been generally respectful.

"I remember I got the shock of my life when we first came to this country and some children picked my flowers without asking," she said. "In England it would be absolutely sacrilege, and children would know that. You would be intruding on someone else's space. Of course, the way Americans landscape their front yards is so different than in England. Over there, they're fenced off or hedged off, by and large. So it's much more private."

Judy's front fence is more ornament than barrier. Even so, her garden in St. Paul is "very like" one she could find in England. "Oh, very like," she said. "I've discovered that many of the plants we grow here—peonies, roses, phlox, delphiniums—are ones I knew all my life. They just have a shorter growing season in Minnesota. Here, the daffodils can be up, out, and over in a day. In England they last for weeks."

Her garden is very informal—again, in the English tradition. "It isn't in rows or formal parterres like the French," she observed. "It's arranged in curves, with nothing set out in rigid patterns. There are clusters of things, with interesting textures. That's what appeals to me." The pinks, blues, and purples she prefers are favorites in England as well. "Also, I do like a certain neatness about the garden and that probably comes from my heritage."

There are things she can't have here, old stone walls, for instance, or roses clambering over the house. And she's given up on a lawn. "The English can be very fastidious about their lawns," she explained. "But it's so much easier there. They don't have drought, they don't have the heat. For me, it would take so much in the way of chemicals that I'm content with my creeping Charlie."

Judy's ideal remains her mother's cottage garden in Devonshire. "When my parents arrived, there was just a meadow," she recalled. "But they created the borders, they created the paths, they created the strawberry patch. It was all very charming. I just have a memory of that garden as the epitome of an English garden." Judy's own garden invites the same observation.

Judy's gardens are attractive in all seasons. The arborvitae hedge, which provides such a fine backdrop for daylilies, roses, and cimicifuga, looks wonderful draped with snow.

Karla and Charlie Kiheri

SIMPLY FINNISH

peeding cars and fast-food restaurants make up the world along Interstate Highway 35 south of Duluth. Just a few miles west, down a quiet lane, the traveler enters another world of clear ponds, white birch, and abundant berries. For Charlie Kiheri, a third-generation Finn, and his wife, Karla, who immigrated eleven years ago, the contrast is far from accidental. Here, Charlie and Karla have created a place apart, a bit of Finland in Carlton County, where they live with their children, Heikki and Selja.

"The most important trees Finns have to have in the yard," said Karla, walking around the farm they are restoring, "are those birch trees. There are songs and poems about them. The other 'must' in a Finnish yard is a mountain ash," she said, pointing to the mountain ashes close to the house. "I guess the mountain ash was the only available natural thing in Finland

that bloomed in the spring and had pretty berries. So it was a decorative thing. We didn't plant these birches—they were already here. But we value them so much that we moved the old garage that blocked our view from the house. Now we see those trees and the pond from our living room.

"Another thing about being a Finn, you know, is that we love the trees and woods. It's an important part of you. It's not just flowers and yards, but it's very necessary to have those trees." As Karla spoke, she pointed out the plantings, the old barn, the new sauna, and the original sauna, burned a few years back by renters.

"This homestead is one hundred years old," she explained. "My husband's great-grandparents, the Wihelas, farmed here. That old sauna was the first thing they built. One side was the washing part and on the other there was a little

Karla, about five, sitting among her family's lupines in Finland. Photograph courtesy of Karla Kiheri.

9

According to Karla, Finns must have birches. These white birches create a leafy ceiling with a constant play of light and shadow.

dressing room big enough for a bed. So that was how they lived; they had warmth and they had cleanliness. Charlie's grandpa built this modest, square, typical Finnish house."

Healthy beds of lilies and phlox, peonies and roses, many of them descendants of flowers planted by earlier generations of Charlie's relatives, are growing near the house. Further off, the fields meet the nearby forests. "Charlie's grandmother, Hilda Haapala, planted all these evergreens around the property in a square in the 1930s," Karla said. "After she died, the place was rented out and got in real bad shape. But even when we saw it empty and neglected, those evergreens gave a cozy feeling. We plant every year a few more trees, and people say, 'You have those trees in the wood.' Yes, we do, but we have to plant trees. I don't know why, but it's important."

This area of the state, settled by Finnish immigrants in the late 1800s, looks just like the old country, Kiheri said. "If somebody dropped me here from an airplane, I wouldn't know where I was unless I heard somebody speaking English.

It looks so much like home. This northeastern Minnesota is just like Finland. I can see why they stopped here," she said, speaking of the earlier immigrants. Even today mailboxes bear last names filled with *u*'s and *k*'s—Maki, Jokela, Kujala, Wuori.

The macrolandscape may be a replica of the old country. But recently Karla has realized that the work she and Charlie are doing has made their private landscape more Finnish as well. "Without knowing it, I'm sure that I'm creating things that are so Finnish because they seem so right to me," said Karla. "In my life, we never had any fancy big yards, but there was enough for me to take an interest."

"You had to have those berry bushes," she said, indicating her big patch of gooseberries and currants. "I think it used to be a real good boost to your nutrition, particularly black currants, which were so high in vitamin C. It was my treat as a kid. I don't mind the sour taste, and I eat them like other people eat chips.

"Of course, I had to start planting roses, just any rose, because that's what I was used to seeing. Already growing by the house were the Hansa rose and the Juhannus rose,

11

that white rose of summer. Every Finn here has one. Somebody probably brought over the cutting from the old country. And when it blooms, you know, it reminds me of home. It smells so good, and it makes me think, oh, it's that time of year again. I'm not missing home, but seeing it bloom is a little bit like when they're playing *Finlandia* on the radio."

Lawns are less important to Finns than to Americans, Karla said. "Finns do want to have that background of green, but our lawns are not so manicured," she explained. "Everybody leaves them seminatural. If you are not living in town, you can't tell where the yard is ending and woods starting. It's like our place here, you know."

The Kiheris' flower boxes are traditional, too, "but they are not as fancy as Austria's or Switzerland's," said Karla. "They are more modest. I think everything in Finland is modest. In the old days, they couldn't afford fancy things, but even now they stay modest." Clearly, Finns resist showy and artificial-looking displays. Their gardens are unostentatious, like themselves.

Karla has carried her garden indoors. On deep sills her ferns

The sauna was often the first structure built by Finnish immigrants. Framed by old-fashioned phlox, the Kiheris' sauna is handsome as well as functional.

and ivy thrive; room-sized ficus, parlor palm, and umbrella tree have turned the living area into a conservatory. "Finns are a little bit gloomy people," she said in explanation, "a little bit melancholy— those dark nights and long winters. If they find that a green plant is a cheering thing, which they do, they have to have something

growing, no matter how wilted and miserable it is."

One important addition to their landscape has been the large, clear pond, Karla said. The area had been swampy and the Kiheris had it dug out, intending to create a wildlife pond. "We found it was fed by cold springs, so it's been excellent for swimming, if you don't mind the cold," she said. "It stays clean and it's pleasing to look at." Describing the pond as "pleasing to look at" is an understatement. The clear blue water framed by tall cattails and birches is what gives the Kiheris' property its serene, retreat-like quality. The visitor has the feeling that this is a complete world, with woods, water, and fields.

Friends and neighbors observing the Kiheris' landscaping over the years—trees planted, pond dug, garage moved, gardens started, house painted—sometimes ask, "Do you think you'll get your money back?" The question makes no sense to Karla and Charlie. "No, nobody ever is thinking that way—it's just home, not an investment," said Karla. "I think Finns feel that yard and home is a relationship that is meant for life. It's your home, and that includes the yard and it's your very own private thing. I don't know if it runs in your genes or if it's something you learn. But just this summer Heikki said, 'Mom, hopefully when we are gone, whoever moves here won't cut the trees down.' He was thinking ahead like that."

Karla wants to be connected to nature, indoors and out. Charlie has enlarged the windows in the house; trees and shrubs have been planted so they can be seen from inside. "I want to see something pretty from every window, even the kitchen," Karla said. "And when I sit on that enclosed porch in the wintertime and the snowflakes are coming down around, it's like a fairyland. Those little joys make a life.

"That beauty of nature is everything. Nothing can compete. So that vine on the house wall is definitely prettier than any siding they can sell. I really want to observe the growing and the changing of the seasons. Even though you know that the season comes to an end, there's the hope of it coming back next spring, and maybe it will be even better."

Philippe Gallandat

BLACK CURRANTS AND WINDOW BOXES

hilippe Gallandat can speak in great detail about the technical requirements of pruning—when to do the work, where to make the cuts, which tools to use. He can explain the horticultural needs of roses and the preferred methods of planting. In fact, Philippe, a native of the French-speaking region of Switzerland, has undergraduate and advanced degrees in horticulture and agriculture. Currently he works in the profession, designing and installing landscapes and maintaining gardens.

But conversations with Philippe are more likely to concern the satisfactions and aesthetics of gardening than the specific how-tos. Speaking in the soft cadences of his native French, he discussed pruning: "When I prune, I revive. There's something magical that happens. It's not just repetitive. There's something very reflective about it. It's like repairing something."

Philippe grew up surrounded by beauty. He observed it in the Swiss landscapes, in his family's large gardens, and even in the way food was prepared. "My mother would apologize," he said, "if she sometimes, sometimes, served something that wasn't presented 'just so.'"

"We were just average people," he added, "but I had a privileged life because the property we rented and the areas around us were just beautiful. We lived on a farm with rose gardens, lawns, boxwood hedges, specimen trees, arbors, and vegetables. There were wonderful stone fences and terraces. There was a little forest with walks in it. It was just beautiful. So that's where I got my interest in farming and gardening."

"You see all that," he continued. "And that's what you know. So it comes naturally to me to present things in a beautiful way."

Gallandat's family lived in the United States when he was a

Gallandat, at fourteen in the garden, with zinnias in front and mountains behind. Photograph courtesy of Philippe Gallandat.

Gallandat enjoys incorporating food plants as ornamentals in his gardens. Here he's growing beans in the window boxes along with the impatiens and heavily scented candlestick vine.

toddler. "My parents came to New York for nine months when I was three years old," he recalled. "Later, I always used to talk about America to my friends at school. It seemed like a big deal. And I would pretend that I could speak with an American accent. I always knew I would come back. It is such

a huge country and there are huge possibilities here."

As a young man he returned for a visit in 1974, but the visit stretched on. "I remember saying to my folks that I wanted to stay at least five years to really experience the country," he recalled. "That five years became eight." Explaining his initial

motives, Philippe observed, "There was a Swiss mentality that I didn't care for. The flip side of everything being neat and tidy is that the people seem somewhat rigid."

Philippe remembers arriving at the decision to stay. "Suddenly I just said, 'I'm here,' and I stopped buying appliances with dual

16

voltages." The decision was like marriage, he reflected. "Making up your mind changes the way you look at things. You've made a commitment; you're not just visiting."

Though he immigrated, Gallandat has maintained continuous ties with Switzerland. "I'm always torn about whether I want to go back or not," he said. "When I go to Switzerland now, people call me 'the American.'" His affection for the European lifestyle and the physical beauty of Switzerland is strong and may call him back yet. "I'm considering retiring there," he said.

Meanwhile, Philippe has brought elements of his homeland to St. Paul. They are obvious in the landscapes he prefers. "Swiss gardens are distinctive in several ways," he explained. "You see a lot of fountains everywhere, even in new buildings. And there are flower boxes on many houses and buildings. Everyone has flowers."

Here, most of the gardens he designs feature handsome, wooden window boxes filled with lush plantings. One of the first renovations he made to his own, recently bought bungalow was to place a set of window boxes along the south wall. "I like most flowers," he said. "I love any spring bulb, especially muscari. My taste is for simple flowers, light ones, ferny ones. So I love astilbe and bleeding heart. And the single zinnia is so pretty."

A characteristic element of the Swiss landscape is the use of natural stone, Philippe explained. "There are beautiful old walls and walks everywhere," Philippe said. "Terraces are made from various kinds of slate and pavers. Sections of the garden are divided off with stone." Not surprisingly, his Minnesota gardens usually feature stone as well. He loves working with it, fitting the pieces together. "A lot of my designs use stone," he said. "People ask how I have a good knack for constructing with it. To me it's inbred, almost. I grew up around it. If you look at pictures of Switzerland, you see stone all over."

A master scrounger, he keeps an eye out for old bricks and pavers.

Philippe often places stone and bricks in the landscapes he designs. Stonework was a feature of most of the Swiss landscapes he observed growing up.

BLACK CURRANTS
(Ribes nigrum)

Beloved all over Europe, black currants *(Ribes nigrum)* were outlawed in America from early in this century until the mid-1960s because they host a virus damaging to white pine. Now rust-resistant varieties of pine have been developed, and interest in the berries has been revived. They are a major crop in France and are the essential ingredient in the liqueur *crème de cassis.* Currant bushes are very prolific and extremely hardy; even the blossoms that appear in early spring withstand the frosts that destroy the flowers of other fruits. Though grown successfully almost to the Arctic Circle, they are at their best when the soil is moist and the air cool and humid. The fruit is used in jams, desserts, cordials, and wine, and the leaves are brewed as tea. Full of vitamin C, black currant tea is given for colds, sore throats, and hoarseness, while the fruit pulp is used in facial masks.

"These are wonderful," he said, pointing to an enormous pile of worn, deep-red bricks. "I love giving new life to old things." Collecting mushrooms recently, Philippe found a rounded, flat stone. "This will make an interesting fountain with just the right base," he said, already envisioning the rock in its future setting.

Because food preparation is an art and a passion in Switzerland, Philippe explained, many Swiss grow their own produce. Unlike in the United States, where the vegetable plot is usually relegated to the backyard, Swiss gardeners grow their vegetables mixed with flowers in the front of the house. Frequently, they will include small fruits. "Having them in front gives easy access," he said. "My mother, just before dinner, would run out and get a bit of basil or chives to cut into the salad. Of course, this makes a huge difference in the way food tastes."

From this experience has come Philippe's philosophy of garden design. "The vegetables are not just hidden," he said. "You see that they are decorative." So, a grape arbor is not simply utilitarian, but handsomely designed and placed as an archway in the garden. Blueberries and currants are integrated into the landscape as ornamentals, with flowers and ground covers around them. "Of course, herbs are always attractive," Philippe said. "And their scents add much to the garden. When our cat brushes against the basil, she will smell of basil for a while." There are always strawberries and raspberries in his garden, along with the Swiss favorite, black currants. "You haven't lived," he said, "until you've tasted black currants."

But Philippe has brought something more subtle than a preference for stone and black currants to his American gardens: old world craftsmanship. It shows in his respect for the materials he uses, in his attention to detail, and in his insistence on seeing a job through from beginning to end.

He has no sense of urgency in finishing a project, even the large job he faces in turning the sparse yard of his new bungalow into a working garden. Each aspect is interesting and worth the necessary time—imagining the possible, finding the right construction materials

Even Gallandat's vegetable garden has visual interest. A trellis for the tomatoes gives height; celosia and marigolds add color.

and plants, reworking the landscape. A tree is not just sheared, but trimmed to recover its natural shape. Stones are not lined up hurriedly; patterns and sizes are selected with care.

"The greatest satisfaction in gardening is peace, mental peace.

There is something very contemplative about it. I'm trying to revisit my childhood with this garden," Philippe explained, looking around at the cleared earth and the flats of flowers waiting to be planted. "I think that is what we all do through life."

Hulya Dortay McCaffrey

DAISIES AND GRAPE LEAVES

n Turkey everybody is into flowers," said Hulya Dortay McCaffrey, with a trace of a Turkish accent, "especially in our city Istanbul. The city is bigger than New York, and people are living in huge, tall apartments. But even way up they have gardens. They're not large, but they have balconies filled with potted plants. So everybody has something in their windows and balconies. You're surrounded by flowers."

Hulya's verbal sketch of Istanbul could well describe her own garden in Minneapolis, where she and her husband, Michael, are "surrounded by flowers." On a modest city lot, Hulya has reserved smallish rectangles of green in her front and back yards; the remainder is filled with annuals and perennials, vines and herbs. Window boxes, hanging baskets, a boulevard bed, and a small pool extend her garden space. "I grow pretty much everything," she said.

Considering the size of her lot and the fact that the brightest spots get only four hours of sunlight, Hulya's garden is diverse. There are several herbs—mint, oregano, basil, thyme, and parsley—to supply her kitchen. "I love herbs," she said. "I just spread them all over wherever I can find room." She grows a few peppers, including Turkish banana peppers, sweet and hot. "These are a lot different than the regular ones," she pointed out. "Their texture is not hard like the ones you find here, and they are tastier. A friend brought the seeds to me."

She has two healthy grapevines, which do at least triple duty. "I got a lot of grapes early in the season," she said, "but the birds got in and took most of the rest. And I've made a batch of vinegar. Actually, I use the vine mostly for the leaves, which I stuff."

McCaffrey uses her own leaves because they're clean and have not

Hulya, at about two and a half, standing among her mother's roses in Istanbul. Photograph courtesy of Hulya Dortay McCaffrey.

Hulya likes daisies and all their look-alikes. Even her window boxes contain the daisylike fan flower (Scaveola) *along with the verbena.*

been sprayed. "You can freeze them, but I usually use them all before winter," she said. Her time-consuming but tasty recipes, which start with a base of rice, olive oil, onion, and mint, are always a hit with guests. "You can include ground meat if you like and other seasonings," Hulya explained, "but the olive oil is essential. You know, olive oil is healthy for you. Now some people don't even like to use that. But if you don't use enough, you won't get any flavor, and it keeps the stuffing moist."

If she had more room, Hulya would grow "this weed that Americans hate, dandelions. It's so good for you. Oh, we have a lot of gypsies in our country. In the summer that's all they sell. But our dandelion is different than the American one; it is not bitter. Once in a while, I get out into the country here to pick it early in the season—then it's good. I boil it a few minutes, rinse in cold water, and dress it with olive oil, lemon juice, mint, and garlic. That's wonderful."

Of all her garden plants, Hulya's favorites are the flowers. "I can't live without flowers, flowers," she said, somewhat amazed at her own attachment. "They are my everything. Even in the wintertime I have blooming plants inside—hydrangea, African violets, and impatiens. It's unbelievable how much enjoyment I get from them. There's nothing in this world I'd rather do than work out here," she said, gesturing to a backyard and deck filled with color even at the season's end. "In fact, we almost missed a plane recently because of this garden. I had to tie up all my plants, about 150 to 200 of them, after a storm."

Though she loves them all, daisies are dearest to her heart. "If it were up to me, I would have all daisies, but my husband wants more of a variety," she said, pointing out the many daisies and look-alikes she cultivates. "Back home, the mountains are carpeted with tiny white and yellow daisies. They are the first flower of spring, and they just cover the ground." In Minnesota, Hulya raises Shasta, Dahlberg, painted, and oxeye daisies, plus other members of the

The McCaffreys' pond has added the gentle sound of water and the hypnotic movement of fish to their garden.

23

Compositae family—cornflowers, asters, and coneflowers.

McCaffrey traces her fascination with flowers to childhood, when she loved to examine the potted plants in her neighbors' gardens. Even now she is slightly surprised at the intensity of her childhood interest. "When I was a little girl, like three or four years old," she recalled, "I used to see other people's flowerpots and bring them home. I didn't hurt them, but I took them without asking. I would put them in my room and I would just sit there and look at them. They were so fascinating to me. After a while I would take them back. One time I got caught and my mother punished me."

Later memories include her family's gardens. "My whole family was interested," she said. "My grandmother and mother both gardened, and my father is a wonderful gardener. My parents live in an apartment, but my father made sure the first floor has a lot of space where he can plant flowers. He's downstairs all the time working with his

Hulya makes fine use of her modest-sized lot with potted plants, bird feeders, urns, and trellising.

plants and his garden is gorgeous. My husband thought that someone professional was doing it."

When Hulya first arrived in Minnesota in the 1970s, she saw a landscape drastically different from her homeland. "There were no gardens here," she said. "It was just flat land, just green. You could see a few flowers here and there. And I was thinking, 'Why is there all this grass? Why can't they grow vegetables and flowers?' That was the first thing we did, put in a garden. Now in the last ten years, everybody is into it, and you see flowers everywhere."

Though she works long hours in her garden, Hulya doesn't strive for formal perfection. "You know, nobody in Turkey sits down and draws a garden plan, saying, 'I'll put this here and something else there.' No, we just mix things up. Most people know their plants real well, how tall they will get, how much space they need. So they plant and know that later they can change things around. I do this also, place things close together and transplant them the next year if I like."

From observing her family, McCaffrey learned to be attentive to her plants and soil. Even on her lunch hour, she runs home to check on things. Whenever possible, she works for hours at a time, pruning and watering. "If you water early in the morning and again late in the afternoon, you will get better results," she advised.

She considers her knowledge about soil one of the most important lessons she learned in Turkey. "You should refresh your soil every two years," she explained. "That's what my mother used to do. That's what my dad and other Turks I know do as well. It makes sense to me, too.

"You know how old dirt looks gray and dry? Well, in the spring before everything starts coming up, you should loosen the dirt with a garden fork. Of course, make sure you know where all your plants are. Then mix in fresh black dirt, potting soil, and manure. If you can get the real stuff from the farm, so much the better. The first year here, we put on the real stinky stuff. I don't think our neighbors appreciated it, but it made great soil," she said with amusement.

In Turkey, life was lived outside whenever weather permitted. "We had four exact seasons," Hulya added, "so we were able to be in the garden a lot. In Turkey, most everyone owns two houses—one in the country and an apartment in town. I used to go visit my grandma in the mountains. Her whole neighborhood gardened. All we did really was sit in the garden and have picnics. Some neighbors had little streams running through their gardens. We would catch a fish and just fry it there."

Hulya has continued the tradition here. "So this is *my* summer house," she said, indicating the garden and the deck, "and inside is my winter house. When I'm home, I'm outside from six in the morning until ten, ten-thirty at night. I'm always looking to see how many inches everything grows and checking to see if everything is healthy. With so much blooming, we have so many birds and so many butterflies. Nothing makes me happier than to sit out here in the midst of these flowers."

Angie Vesel Smith

SLOVENIAN SWEET PEAS

talk to my flowers," said Angie Vesel Smith, gently touching the pink petunias beneath her kitchen window. "You're supposed to talk to the flowers," she said in the accents of her Slovenian homeland. Perhaps that explains why her gardens look so healthy. Maybe the flowers thrive because she waters them all by hand with a watering can. "The hose is too strong," she said. Most likely everything grows for Angie because she's been gardening seriously since she was fifteen and helping in the family gardens even earlier.

In any case, on this late July day, Angie's beds of petunias—white, pink, fuschia—grow thickly around the house. "They come by themselves," she said, airily dismissing any effort on her part. Vying for attention are the snapdragons, marigolds ("I save the seeds"), and the annual asters, another plant that reseeds itself for her year after

year. By the front door, Angie has urns of geraniums and 'New Guinea' impatiens.

Occupying pride of place are the velvety pink blooms of "Finland Flower," nodding in the summer breeze. "My neighbor gave me these seeds," she said, "but she doesn't remember the name. She calls it 'Finland Flower' because someone brought the seeds from the old country."

Neatly fenced and surrounded by flowers, Angie's vegetables are flourishing in the backyard. She has green peppers and beans, parsley and cabbages. An absolute thicket of tomatoes grows against the north fence. There are hills of potatoes and cucumbers and rows of onions, carrots, and beets ("I like the beets and the tops, too"). A short row of corn grows beside the south fence and two kinds of lettuce grow on a mound in the middle. The tiny leaves of newly planted lettuce are

popping up where the radishes once grew. A plot of garlic is tucked against the back. Nary a weed shows its head.

Bordering the vegetable garden is a riot of colorful annuals and perennials, including sunflowers and the sedum 'Autumn Joy.' The soft, fragrant blooms of sweet peas completely blanket the back fence.

Angie's been gardening for about twenty years in Biwabik. Before that she gardened in Leonidas and West Eveleth, and as a young woman she gardened in Slovenia. Many of the same vegetables and flowers have been in all her gardens, but "everything was bigger

Angie's neatly fenced garden provides enough beans, carrots, beets, and tomatoes for the winter. Even in late summer she's still harvesting produce.

over there," she said, referring to Slovenia. Out in the country were large fields of potatoes, cabbages, and onions. Smaller plots were near the house.

"Here it is so different," she said, explaining the size of the gardens in Slovenia and their importance to the household. "We couldn't just go to the store for everything, so we had to make it all at home. We grew apples and plums. But the plums were juicy and sweet, not like the ones today, so tough you have to cut with a knife. People made whiskey with the fruit. They cooked up the plums and put them in a big barrel to ferment. I didn't ever make it," she said with a laugh, "but I saw people doing it. And they made wine from the apples.

"We had sweet cherries, too. One morning early my brother's wife brought me lots, and I ate and ate them. My mother said, 'Don't eat so many, you might get sick.' Also, there were grapes on an arbor by the house. You could walk under the vines, and the grapes hung down just so," she said, remembering the bunches above her head.

"Around the house there were flowers. Oh my, there were sweet-smelling flowers by the windows. We had such beautiful roses and carnations. We had everything we have here and more, because there the winters were not so cold."

In 1937, when Angie was twenty-five, she left her family and her country with its beautiful gardens and came to America to marry Louis Vesel. "You might say it was an arranged marriage," explained her son Jim. Relatives of her future husband had traveled to Slovenia, met Angie, and suggested she come to Minnesota to marry Louis, who was working for the Oliver Mining Company. "On November 13, 1937, only one month after I got here, we were married," Angie recalled, with the smile of one pleased by the outcome.

The two set up housekeeping in Leonidas and began to garden

SWEET PEAS
(Lathyrus odoratus)

Originally, the sweet pea was a modest wildflower from Italy with small maroon and blue blossoms and an exquisite fragrance. The Italian botanist and priest Franciscus Cupani first described it in 1697, with the classification *lathyrus*, Greek for pea and *odoratus* meaning scented. By 1772 the seeds were available at market, and the flower was described by a nurseryman as "somewhat like honey and a little tending to the orange-flower smell."

Hybridists spent years working to enlarge the flower and to expand the palette of pastels beyond the original blue and maroon. By the Victorian era, no dinner table or wedding bouquet in the United States or England was complete without sweet peas. At the Bi-Centenary Sweet Pea Exhibition in 1900 at the Crystal Palace in London, 264 varieties were on display.

In the first half of this century, hybridists nearly bred the scent out of the flower in their search for large blossoms. Fortunately, many of the older lines survived, saved by home gardeners like Angie, and these have been recently offered to the public. These heirlooms are not only more fragrant, but are more tolerant of heat.

Sweet peas form a fragrant fence around Angie's garden.
She saves her seeds from year to year.

together. Even as their three sons arrived, Angie and her husband raised enough vegetables to supply their growing family. Many of the lessons she had learned in Europe worked well in Minnesota. "In Slovenia, from the age of fifteen I worked for a relative for ten years, doing the gardening. In fact, I did almost everything except cut the grass. They had a scythe, and I wouldn't use that," she said with a laugh. "But even when I was younger, I helped my mother with our vegetables."

Though Angie's garden here is smaller than its Slovenian counterpart, there are many similarities, she said. The visitor first notices its beauty. This is no flat, weedy vegetable patch, but a lovingly tended garden. An attractive metal fence with a small gate allows Angie to get in and keeps stray animals out. The vegetables are growing on softly mounded rows with paths in between. "My son tills this for me in spring, and then I shape up the rows with my hands," she said. Rather than being all parallel, the rows of vegetables make a tidy patchwork pattern. At the front, a carefully painted Madonna is

Petunias and annual asters grow thickly against the house. They both reseed themselves every year.

nestled among the petunias and marigolds.

These are the vegetables Angie knew in the old country, "except for the tomatoes," she said. "There were no tomatoes over there." From a plot about twenty-four feet square, she raises enough to supply

her for most of the year. "It's nice to get something fresh," she said.

Just as her parents did, Angie stores vegetables for the winter. "I dry the onions on a table in the garage," she explained. "Then I put them in a box and place it in the cool of the basement. You have

As she has done for as long as she can remember, Angie makes a large batch of sauerkraut every year. "I have to buy the cabbage now, because I don't grow enough," she said, not wanting to take unearned credit. "Then you shred the cabbage fine and put it in a twelve-gallon jar." Angie makes a *lot* of sauerkraut. "Add in caraway seed and a salt brine. Cover it and skim it every day. As long as it's bubbling, the sauerkraut is fermenting. When it stops, you know it's ready."

Angie saves most of her flower seeds—the marigolds, zinnias, snapdragons, and sweet peas. "The sweet peas grow so thick," she explained, "because I just throw on extra seed." She brings in her geraniums every fall and puts them in the basement for winter. In February she starts to water them again, so they'll be ready for the outdoors come summer.

Angie is an expert in the "old ways," but she makes great use of her modern appliances, too. "We used to can in Slovenia, and we canned here in Minnesota," she said. "I still can beets, but now I preserve some of my vegetables in the freezer. My tomatoes I cook and

then strain—it's almost like a sauce. Then I freeze them.

"I put parsley, too, in the freezer and some I dry in the microwave," she said, pulling a jar of fragrant, home-dried parsley off the shelf. "After washing it, you put it on a paper plate and cover with a paper towel. Then you dry it in the microwave. Mine is not a very powerful oven, so I dry it about ten minutes. Then I crumble it and save it in a jar. It's good to add to the soup."

Angie admits that she doesn't "cook like she used to," when she was feeding a full house. Still, she makes her own pasties, pies, soups, and noodles, prepared with farmfresh eggs from her son's hens. There's usually enough to give away to family and friends.

Though her garden is productive and beautiful, "it's not that much work," said Angie. "Besides, I like working outside. I like to see how everything grows. First thing, when I wake up in the morning, I have to look out my kitchen window and see my plants."

to cover it and make sure no light gets in, then they will last for months. Oh, I like to have onions for my cooking." Her potatoes and carrots are stored in much the same way. Even in late July she is still eating carrots from last year's garden.

Joseph Braeu

FINE GERMAN CRAFTSMANSHIP

he maxim, "If you would know the man, know the boy," could have been inspired by nurseryman Joe Braeu of Duluth, who as a boy in southern Germany spent every spare moment in his family gardens. Today Joe and his wife, Debbie, operate Edelweiss Nursery, selling trees, shrubs, herbs, and perennials. Joe has an enormous selection of hard-to-find plants, expanding the choices usually found in northern Minnesota. The business provides a broad range of services for clients, from planting advice to complex landscaping.

Although Braeu (pronounced "Broy") enjoys the whole operation, he takes greatest pleasure in designing. His style is distinctive— "You can always recognize one of Joe's landscapes," Debbie said. The gardens include a felicitous mix of conifers, grasses, succulents, shrubs, and trees, with intriguing shapes and colors (he likes contorta witch

hazel, Japanese hydrangea vines, European larch, azaleas, and rhodo-dendrons), and perennials of all kinds. He loves using heaths and heathers, which bloom on and on. For whimsy, Joe will add a bit of to-piary or a weeping birch or juniper.

During his boyhood in Germany, Joe grew vegetables in the family's large community plot (the *scherber-garten*), where they all worked on planting and weeding. The area around Bad Sackingen, his home-town, usually had plentiful rainfall, but the family devised a labor-intensive system for the dry times. "We had a wine barrel on a wagon, and we made a bucket brigade, going down to dip water out of the Rhine," Joe recalled. "We never thought about how much work it was—we just did it. I always thought it was fun because I got to ride down in the wagon."

His grandfather was a masterly fruit grower, and Joe loved following

At age ten, Joe stands with his sister, Kathy, by the espaliered pear tree at his grandfather's house. Photograph courtesy of Joseph Braeu.

33

Joe creates interesting groupings on his nursery grounds to give home owners design ideas. Here the bright yellow of golden privet and golden barberry contrast with the deep green of weeping larch and the gray of artemisia 'Silver Broach.'

him around. "My grandparents had a really beautiful garden," he recalled, "with raspberries, cherries, and against the house were espaliered pear and apple trees. He taught me to take care of all that. He also was into beekeeping and sometimes I got to help harvest the honey. He smoked this awful, skinny cigar that almost killed me, but it kept the bees out of your face."

A favorite plot was his own bit of ground in the backyard. There, Joe used to "move earth around, dig streams, make little castles, add rocks and plants." It was his own miniature world. "I did a lot of playing out there. I never knew it would lead to a life of this," he said, gesturing at the display gardens around Edelweiss.

Indeed, horticulture was not Joe's first career choice. "In Germany, when you're fourteen," he explained, "you make a decision to continue school or choose a trade. I wanted to be an auto mechanic, because I liked to work with my hands." When a test showed less-than-perfect hearing, Joe was forced to go another route. (At the time, mechanics needed to listen to the engine.) "My mother reminded me that I'd always

loved plants and being outside. She was right," he said.

In the course of his horticultural classes and apprenticeship, Braeu learned the floral and nursery trades. One job took him to a cemetery, landscaping individual graves. "German cemeteries are not like those in the United States," he emphasized. "They're beautiful. Each little grave site is its own small garden. Families keep them tended or hire gardeners to design them. That's how I learned to do miniature plots. I used thyme, salvia, boxwood, and dwarf conifers. Just recently my old mentor there told me that people always praised my designs. I never knew that—I just loved doing them."

Germany gave Joe a rich horticultural background, but by age eighteen, he was ready to move on. "I was never one to accept the status quo," he said, "but always asked questions and was a little rebellious. I wondered what else the world had to offer."

Aiming to travel around the world, he headed to Sweden, Denmark, and later Canada, working in the floral, greenhouse, and nursery trades at each stop. On a

Soft lamb's ears, spiky liatris, and mounds of lady's mantle are framed by low patches of creeping thyme.

trip to the United States, he met Debbie and his traveling came to an end. In 1977 they married and moved to Duluth. There, with the help of an old pickup truck and a few tools, the couple started a modest yard maintenance business. Soon people began to ask for design help with their gardens.

With the fresh eye of an outsider, Joe could see that most Duluth landscapes were drawn from the same basic plan—a smooth lawn and foundation plantings around the house. "At first, I thought you could only grow a few plants in Duluth—spirea and arborvitae," Joe said. As one predisposed to question the status quo, he wondered why.

In Germany, Joe had been involved with intimate, idiosyncratic landscapes. These diverse gardens provided fruit or vegetables for the family, gave opportunities for creating beauty, or offered chances for recreation. Men like his grandfather took pride in their espaliers and grafts. Others grew herbs and exotic plants. Their gardens were meant to be used and enjoyed.

Joe began to suggest alternatives to his clients, such as adding perennials and grasses to the shrubs

DWARF CONIFERS

Confronted with space constraints, the ancient Japanese collected and preserved small and unusual varieties that occasionally appeared among their conifers. They used them to create representations of natural scenes within the limited space of their gardens. Similarly, American and European gardeners have begun to use these dwarfs because of the way they add interest to small residential and commercial properties.

Dwarf conifers originate in several ways: by genetic mutation, as stunted tissue (witches' brooms), and as low, weak-growing shoots. Nursery professionals propagate these conifers to create attractive shrubs with a multitude of foliage colors, textures, and growth habits.

Dwarf and slow-growing conifers

("That's done very much in Germany," he said) and using plants with unusual coloration or shape. When he was unable to find certain plants in the area, he traveled to large growing ranges in Oregon. "He was like a kid in a candy store," said Debbie.

The couple realized they needed to stock and sell the plants they liked, so in 1985 they bought property north of town, naming it Edelweiss. There, Joe could collect the hard-to-find conifers and shrubs he admired, testing the plants for hardiness in Minnesota weather. When told by a nursery supplier that magnolias would not survive Duluth winters, Joe became intrigued. He has since successfully tested magnolias (he recommends five selections), heaths and heathers, and evergreen rhododendrons. "I'll try anything three times," he said, "after that, it's out."

At Edelweiss, Joe could create gardens to showcase his ideas. He placed an alpine garden at the road, and heathers and heaths up the driveway. At the front entrance, he added a seating area, brick walkway, and perennial bed. Neighbors wondered as the Braeus removed all their sod. "At that time, nobody here was planting front-yard gardens," said Joe. "I used to wonder why I did things a certain way in my landscapes. But when I was in Germany a few years back, I would notice plantings and realize 'Oh, that's where that comes from.'"

As word of his style has spread, Joe has been able to spend more time on his first love, designing. Leave to others the detailed plans and drawings—Joe designs by hand. "When I go out to give an estimate," he explained, "I'll give them the feeling of what it will look like. Now a lot of my clients give me free rein."

Joe is a happy man. "My avocation and my vocation are the same," he said. "And I make a lot of other people happy. It's a great job when you can accomplish a lot and be satisfied with what you have."

HARVESTING JOY

Tae Young Lee, Samup Chang, Myong Lee, and Bokson Pyunn

WILD SESAME AND BALLOON FLOWER

Walking from high-rise to garden, one passes the all-too-typical urban scene—busy parking lot, unkempt knoll, massive concrete overpass. So the bright green tapestry of thirty-three vegetable plots is doubly unexpected. Clustered together, the lovingly tended gardens are bursting with produce even on this early June afternoon.

Besides the familiar chives, onions, many-hued lettuces, and numerous peppers, there are low clumps of watercress and rows of Chinese bellflower, harvested for its roots after three years. Americans know the plant as balloon flower *(Platycodon grandiflora)* and grow it only for the purple and white blossoms. The matte green of wild sesame plants *(Perilla frutescens),* grown for leaf and seed, contrasts with shiny spinach and chard. Tropical-looking taro *(Colocasia esculenta),* used for its tuber in soup, stands stiffly above ground.

Hugging the earth is the pale green vine, *toduk (Codonopsis pilosula),* which yields a white root for stir-fries. Artfully improvised structures—trellises constructed of old branches, sheds of found wood, gates made of bits of metal and plastic—add a suggestion of sculpture to the garden.

The Korean Peace Garden is planted and tended by thirty-three Korean elders (ages sixty to ninety) of the Cedar-Riverside apartments in Minneapolis. It is an "amazing garden," said program coordinator Kwangja Kwon of the Korean Volunteer Services Office. "This gardening," she said, "is their life."

The garden started seven years ago because many of the elders had been farmers in their home country and "they missed their farms," Kwon said. "Their children came to this country first, and then they invited their parents. But life here is hard for them. They don't know English very well, and they are living in the high-rise by themselves."

Some began planting small patches around the complex, but other residents complained. With the help of John Fabian, manager of the apartment complex, and permission from the city, the Koreans were given a grassy area a short walk from the high-rise.

The spot turned out to be full of rocks, but the elders began digging with hand tools. "It was a really tough job, but they were happy," said Kwon. "They were enjoying the digging, even though they had difficulty getting out all the rocks, because they had hope."

Once the ground was cleared, the elders dug in compost they had made. In later years they've continued to add compost and manure from the University of Minnesota's agriculture campus. "Now they have really good soil," Kwon said. "They plant lots of things, not only for eating fresh, but also to save a lot of food money. Besides, they can't find a lot of this in the stores. They grow many rare things."

These rare plants have special meaning to Koreans, Kwon pointed out. The *suk (Artemisia vulgaris)*, for example, is added to soup and salad, but is also used to give a pleasant green tint to food. "It is herbal medicine, too. Elders like to put it in the bath water because it makes the skin so smooth. It also speeds the healing of new mothers, they believe," she said.

Taro is the principal ingredient of *Toran gak*, taro soup. The soup is an essential dish served at the yearly Full Moon festival, August 15.

In the midst of urban congestion, Korean elders have created gardens of beauty and utility.

Since taro is a tropical plant, gardeners must nurture it indoors during the long Minnesota winter.

Toduk (Codonopsis pilosula), a climbing herb with a lovely, bell-shaped flower, is eaten to increase vital energy. An old Korean story tells of the *toduk* root, explained Kwon. "There was once a father who was seriously ill. No medicine could cure him, so his daughter went out searching for *toduk*. Only those who have care and respect for their father can find this plant," related Kwon. "Otherwise, it is invisible. But this girl loved her father very much, so she found the root and gave it to him to eat. After that he was cured."

Chinese bellflower (Platycodon grandiflora), *also known as balloon flower, is important to Korean cooks for its edible root.*

FOR FIVE YEARS, Bokson Pyunn has grown many vegetables in her plot, including those she doesn't see at the market. There are chives and green and multiplier onions, of course, but also hot peppers and the Korean favorite, wild sesame. Grown from seed saved over the winter, these robust plants have leaves and seeds with the flavor of cumin and a hint of cinnamon. Adding a bright yellow color to the rows are the flowers of crown daisy *(Chrysanthemum coronarium),* or *Ssukat* in Korean. The young leaves and stems give a tangy taste to Bokson's stir-fries and casseroles.

Bokson grows a Korean zucchini that she finds more flavorful than the one generally available in American groceries. Like its Italian counterpart, the Korean zucchini is versatile. Bokson uses it in soup and in noodle dishes. One favorite dish is zucchini pancakes, made of sliced zucchini, egg, and onion, shaped into a patty and fried.

Like most Koreans, Pyunn prefers the *homi,* the short-handled hoe with the triangular blade, for hand weeding. To use it, she must be flexible and kneel or hunker close to the ground. In addition, she works with standard American equipment, such as rakes, shovels, and hoes.

IT'S EASY TO picture strong, cheerful Samup Chang working in the wholesale fish business, as she did in Korea. She was a "busy woman and had no time to

Codonopsis pilosula, a climbing herb with bell-shaped flowers, is grown for its root. Used as food and medicine, the plant figures in Korean tales, giving strength to the weary.

garden," she said. Besides, she lived on the ocean, where the soil was sandy and "the wind full of salt."

"Now I have time," she said, "and I am growing the vegetables that I love—bellflower root, watercress, wild sesame. I can stop by any time and take care of the plants and get pleasure from the garden."

Chang and the other elders begin work as soon as the snow melts, even if it's cold. They work the ground in April and plant cool-weather crops. Some of their vegetables are left in the ground over the winter, so the seeds will germinate early and get a head start.

Samup knows that gardening is good for her health. "Vegetables are strong," she said by way of explanation. "They're growing. I want to be strong. So I take care of myself."

MYONG LEE'S girlish demeanor gives no clue to her strength and determination. Her twenty-by-ten-foot plot contains twenty-five different kinds of plants and nary a weed. Perhaps that's because she spends "the whole day in the garden." She grows two kinds of lettuce and three kinds of beans ("short, long, and red," she said). There are two types of green

onions, as well as cabbage, radishes, and the Korean favorites—Chinese bellflower, wild sesame, and *Ssukat* with its yellow flower.

Lee didn't garden much in Korea because she was too busy in the house. But after moving to Minnesota, she observed others gardening. "I see what they are doing," she said, "and I do the same way." It is the same way, perhaps, but also Myong's way. She has become an expert gardener, raising buckets of produce the last four years. Even in early June, she says, she is eating "many things" from her garden.

By necessity, she has become something of a handywoman, building trellises, a shed, and other furnishings for her apartment and the garden. "She builds everything there," Kwon said. "She gathered wood and sticks and made a little storage building and also the gate around the garden."

TAE YOUNG LEE insists that he is eighty, but his lean face and firm voice are those of a fit sixty-year-old. He has farmed and gardened most of his life—perhaps that has kept him young. Lee had a large farm near Seoul; the garden was "his living," and provided for the education of his ten children ("they are all successful in the United States," he interjected). In his country he had animals and grew rice, vegetables, and "many peppers—the basic ingredient in most Korean food."

Compared to his farm, Lee's garden here is "just a little spot," he said modestly, "really not much space at all." In fact, he grows a number of very healthy crops to feed himself and his wife, and to share with his children. Wild sesame, balloon flower, and *toduk*,

are there, of course, plus "Korean-style peppers that are not that hot and not that mild." He raises cucumbers for his wife's pickles and a zucchini-shaped eggplant, grown for its stems as well as its fruit.

Carefully tended Napa cabbages figure prominently in his wife's *kimchi*, the Korean pickle that is served at every meal. There are "many, many recipes for *kimchi*," explained Kwon, depending on the personality of the cook. Lee's wife makes won-

derful *kimchi*, Kwon said. "We all look forward to the samples she brings to the office."

About farming, Lee said, he had no choice—it was "a living." But gardening is his passion. "Whenever I wake up in the morning, I can't wait," he said. "I have to come out and look at everything in the garden the first thing; after that I can eat breakfast. I like to be in the garden—that is how I like to spend my time."

WILD SESAME
(*Perilla frutescens*)

The aromatic annual, wild sesame (also called 'Beefsteak Plant') resembles basil. Its wrinkled, purple foliage has a pleasant cinnamon-mint smell. A member of the mint family, wild sesame has the characteristic square stems and four stamens of most species in that family. The plant, which grows about three feet high and bears pink flowers in late summer, was popular in American gardens as an ornamental until coleus took its place in the early 1900s.

In Asia the wild sesame is much used as a medicine for flu, lung ailments, restless fetus, and incorrect energy balance. The foliage provides a red food coloring and an antimicrobial substance to pickled foods. Koreans extract oil from the seeds for cooking, as well as for industrial uses. In Japan the leaves, seeds, and flower spikes are a basic culinary herb, *shisho*.

Perilla frutescens. *Photograph by David Cavagnaro.*

Alida Olson

A FAIRY COTTAGE

lida Olson's friends and relatives would like to see her take it easy. They worry when they see her behind her heavy cultivator, cleaning out the rows in her garden. When she spends all day mowing her big country yard, they ask why she works so hard. "Well," she replies, "I don't get tired." Every year when Alida plants dahlias and gladioli, her friends suggest that she drop such labor-intensive gardening. "You see," she said with a girlish laugh, "I never get tired of hoeing around."

After all, Alida is ninety-five. Most people her age are slowing down. Not Alida, who's up at six to get her housework done, maintain her large gardens, and cook three meals a day. Repairmen, mail carriers, and friends have learned that Alida always has coffee and cookies ready, and usually a full meal. "O-h-h-h, that mailman has to come all the way down my road," she said in explanation.

Olson is an energetic, generous woman who looks to the future. She can talk about her Norwegian grandparents and their life in the dugout. Strong in her memory is the story of the great storm when the oxen were covered with ice and her grandmother needed twine to get to the barn and back. "Wasn't that something?" she said. "And they called it the good old days." She can tell the tale of her father's arrival in Minnesota from Norway and how he worked on the Jacobsons' (pronounced "Yahcobsons") place for a while. "Everyone around here spoke Norwegian then," she said. "They say they still do up at Starbuck."

But Alida is just as interested and involved in the current life of her community. "O-h-h-h, it's been so much going on in this house, you can't believe it," she said, describing recent bridal showers, church services, and birthday parties. At all

Alida's gardens have always been spectacular. Here, in the 1940s, she stands amid her healthy daisies. Photograph courtesy of Alida Olson.

47

Alida's vigorous stands of love-lies-a-bleeding reseed themselves every year.

these occasions, Alida has contributed cakes and salads, bouquets from the garden, and handmade gifts. Whenever a friend falls sick, Alida is there with one of her prized roses, and perhaps a bit of food. Every Sunday she takes two bouquets to church. "All my life," she said, "two bouquets, because they have to have one on each side. The pastor tells me it's so good to smell garden flowers in church."

Olson takes pleasure in every imaginable circumstance. "Boredom, oh, I don't know what that is. I'm happy if it's bad weather because then I can do my handwork, and I'm happy if it's nice, of course, because then I can go to town. You always need a little something," she said with a giggle.

Of all her joys, the gardens may be her greatest. They surround her indoors and out, pots of flowers up the steps, hanging baskets on the porch, perennial borders along the front of the house, and potted plants in the window. Two large vegetable plots are in the backyard and by the barn. Several oval flower beds are scattered about the lawn. Clustered at the entrance are birdhouses, painted wooden cutouts,

and colorful containers filled with geraniums, petunias, and vines. In the midst of all these blossoms, the small white house with gingerbread trim looks like a fitting residence for a fairy godmother.

Alida has had extensive gardens all her life. Until a few years back, she tended an enormous vegetable plot along the road to her place. "People called it the nursery because it was so big," she explained. The vegetables supplied her parents and her brother, but they were also a significant means of income. Alida sold the produce at the nearby farmers' market in Belgrade. "Oh, I had a cultivator, you know," Alida said, dismissing any suggestion that a lot of work was involved.

"There were always flowers around the place, because Mother loved them," she recalled. "I can just see her in amongst the daisies. My, that was pretty. She loved lilies and daisies." When Alida refers to "the place," she means the original farmstead house, which first belonged to her grandparents. Later she lived there with her parents. After their deaths, she stayed on alone. "This is a Century Farm," she said, pointing out the framed certificate on the wall. "The farm has been in cultivation for over a hundred years."

In 1993 the old house burned, but with her usual spunk, Alida decided to remain on the property. With the help of friends and family, she found a modern rambler for sale, had it moved, dug a basement, and laid a foundation. To keep a connection with the original house, Alida installed the old farm's gin- gerbread trim on her new place and painted the rambler white with blue on the doors and windows.

Because of the construction work, she lost most of the original gardens and had to start over—a daunting task for most gardeners. Alida was ninety-one at the time, but set about preparing the soil and planting seeds or "starts" from friends. Just a few years later, her large beds look as though they've been there for decades. "The soil is better now," she said cheerfully, "because it doesn't dry out so fast with all that clay under it."

GROUND-CHERRIES *(Physalis pruinosa)*

A low, sprawling plant that produces hundreds of cherry-sized, yellow fruits in a paperlike husk, this relative of tomatillos and tomatoes has a sweet citrus flavor. Good in jams, pies, and salads, it can be stored in the husk for several months. Its versatility and heavy production in the first season made it popular with immigrants earlier in Minnesota's history.

PRINCE'S FEATHER *(Polygonum orientale)*

The "giant mutant of the buck- wheat *(Polygonum)* family" is Prince's feather *(Polygonum orientale)*, also called kiss-me-over- the-garden-gate and ladyfingers. From six to eight feet tall, this erect, thick-stemmed plant has dangling, bell-shaped, pink to rose-red or white blooms, which sway in the slightest breeze. The plant self-sows readily, as Alida can attest. Very popular with Victorian gardeners, who fancied the quirky and the novel, Prince's feather almost disappeared from cultivation for the last fifty years. Its vigorous self-sowing ensured its survival and it has begun to appear again in seed catalogs.

Alida's gardens are dramatic— long rows of brilliant cosmos, giant burgundy cockscombs that seed themselves, purple climbing beans, and tall sunflowers. Her vigorous love-lies-a-bleeding, which Alida calls "kiss-me-over-the-garden- gate," commands attention in the side yard. By the house, several enormous plants ("they call them ladyfingers") draw the eye. "These get as tall as the house," Alida said. "People are always asking me what they are." These annuals, with their drooping fuschia flowers, seem to be a giant mutant of the buckwheat *(Polygonum)* family.

Kiss-me-over-the-garden-gate (Polygonum orientale).

Pointing out the special attributes of each plant, Alida often calls attention to its origin as well. "These lace peonies—my friend gave me a start. They're a hundred dollars, I guess, but she got it from her cousin. They look so beautiful in my church bouquets." Or, "I got the start from Mrs. Swanson. She gave me those fuschias and then I took slips and slips. Oh, I got so many."

Olson has gotten many of her plants from others, but she seems to have supplied half the county from her own yard. Any visitor expressing an interest is sure to go home with a flower or two. People are always coming out to dig plants for their own yards. Amazingly, considering her age, Alida still sells her perennials and slips of her annuals. Every Thursday she and her friend Olga head to the Sales Barn in Belgrade with a car full of ferns, hostas, potted plants, and flowers. "They [the customers] meet me at the car when I drive up," she said. "And they always want to know if I have anything new. They tell me, 'When we buy from the greenhouse, it comes up one year and then is dead the next. But when we buy

from you, they grow and grow.' Some of them have so much of my stuff, they call it Alida's Garden.

Alida also sells produce at the Sales Barn. "I don't ask much for it," Alida explained, "because they have tables and tables there." Throughout the summer, she sells carrots, cucumbers, string beans, squash, tomatoes, and peppers. "Olga said, 'Wouldn't it be terrible if they made us take that driving test again?'"

In addition, Alida grows strawberries, raspberries, and ground-cherries *(Physalis pruinosa)* for her own use. "These make such good sauce with a little lemon or orange in it," she said, pulling aside the leaves to reveal the cherry. "When I take a basket to the Sales Barn, they take them right away."

Olson raises three kinds of onions ("white, dark, and multiplier"), corn, and peas. A twenty-foot row of beets makes a decorative border along the side flower bed. "I freeze my beets and then have them all winter," she said. "Take 'em up when they're real young for a good flavor." She has rows of eggplants and cabbages and lets the lettuce go to seed for an early spring crop.

In late August, Alida starts to "put up" her produce. She cans quarts of tomatoes and sauce. "People ask me why I can so many. Well, I say, it keeps in the jars and if we shouldn't get any next year, then I'll still have some." She makes pear sauce and peach sauce to have ready for guests. "I like to have this for my company," she explained.

There's nothing hectic or harried to Alida's life, busy though it is, because she handles her chores with balance and zest. When asked about all the cookies she bakes, for example, she answered, "Oh, I just do them when I'm not busy with something else." And in explaining why dahlias and gladioli weren't a dreaded chore, she said, "Well, I enjoy digging for them because I do it when I know I have time. There isn't any hurry with them, you know, just sometime in the fall, before it gets winter. But to me, doing something with flowers is never unpleasant. It's just fun for me."

Kenrie Williams

AN EDIBLE BACKYARD

"I was born in the wrong era. I should have been a pioneer woman," declared Kenrie Williams, after describing her gardening, canning, and crafting routines. "I don't mind doing hard labor all day long rather than sitting behind a desk because then I know I've accomplished something."

Turning out grapevine wreaths, canning tomatoes, or freezing collards, Kenrie is a lesson to all who claim they have no space or sun. Her small city plot gets "only maybe four hours of direct sunlight, and six to eight hours of diffused light because it's jammed between two houses." Still, she harvests a goodly quantity of produce every summer.

Kenrie raises eggplants, lettuce ("the cut-and-come variety"), and tomatoes enough to eat, can, and freeze. Making the best use of limited space, she plants root crops (beets, carrots) between the rows, and reseeds whenever one crop is done. She has collard and mustard greens, usually getting four pickings from each. "Last year my husband cooked up a stew pot full, and we froze and ate them all winter long," she said with satisfaction.

Williams grows a tier of June-bearing strawberries, which give a healthy crop every summer. She has green peppers and jalapeños. "I try to squeeze in as many of those as possible, 'cause I can and freeze them, too," she said. "I have a no-cook method for the jalapeños. The peppers come out a little softer than I want, but they're good in chili and sauces, and they add zing to a vegetable dish."

In typical Kenrie fashion, she makes her grapevines work triple duty. "Well, first they cover that ugly fence," she said. "They have great foliage, and I thought that even if we never got any grapes, we'd have the leaves and maybe I'd learn to cook with them."

She hasn't. Instead her family eats Concords and something labeled "green" grapes every summer. To keep the neighbor kids away, she's announced that these are "poison" berries. Then in the fall Kenrie harvests the vines, makes wreaths, and sells them—a lot of produce from two-dollar roots.

Making multiple use of a plant fits into Kenrie's scheme for edible landscaping. "I try to encourage people to incorporate different types of vegetables and fruits in amongst the other flowers and things. It's another way to get more gardening space from a smaller yard."

PIGEON PEA
(Cajanus cajan)

Ancient in cultivation, the pigeon pea is an important food in the tropics and subtropics. It is known to have been cultivated in Egypt before 2000 B.C. because seeds were found in the tombs there. It is presumably a native of Africa and was taken later to the Caribbean, where it is still called *Pois Angola*. The fruits, up to three inches long, are produced on shrubs three to ten feet high. The peas may be eaten green, but are often cooked in stews, such as Kenrie describes, or as *dal*, the traditional dish of India.

The pigeon pea is especially useful because of its ability to produce in regions with poor soils and in areas too dry for most other food crops. For this reason, it is favored in arid regions, such as parts of India, the Near East, and some West Indian islands.

How did Williams become a self-described "gardening fiend" when most of her friends "don't want to get their hands dirty"?

"When I was growing up on the island [the Bahamas]," she recalled, "everybody was growing something. Some people grew corn, some grew okra and tomatoes, some grew mangoes. We had an almond tree and a mango and two guava trees. There was a canep (species unknown) and a sapodilla tree (*Manilkara zapota*). That was the hardest to wait for. You could see it on the tree, but it wasn't any good until it was ripe and then it was s-o-o-o sweet.

"You couldn't afford to buy a lot of the stuff you wanted. So you basically grew what you could and got your money's worth out of that. What you didn't eat, you sold to neighbors. We usually did have two or three chickens. They would scratch up the soil and fertilize it, too. Then one or two would disappear in the summer and another one around Christmas. For a time we had a goat for the milk. We ate that, too!"

When Kenrie was nine, the family moved to Florida so her mother could further her education. "She wanted to go to college, more than a two-year college," she explained. "In the Bahamas that's all you were able to achieve." Come summer, Kenrie and her two siblings were sent back to the island to stay with relatives. "We loved it, staying with Aunt Dot, Aunt Althea, and Aunt Doris. I mean, we stayed the *whole* summer."

While in Nassau, Kenrie usually helped relatives with their gardens. Two years stand out vividly in her mind: the two summers when all the cousins helped Aunt Althea and Uncle Dave chip away at the volcanic rock on which their house was built. To hear Kenrie tell it, the work was not so much child labor as high adventure, demonstrating that in communal labor, the emphasis is often on *communal*, not *labor*.

"You know what volcanic rock looks like?" she asked rhetorically. "It's all craters and jagged edges. That was the yard. We couldn't go outside barefoot. If we did, we ended up with rock blisters on our feet. There was no soil anywhere to plant. We spent the summer with a sledgehammer breaking up this rock. If you were too tired or too small to break up rock, you had to tote rock," she said with a laugh.

"So we ended up piling it in the front yard. I remember by midsummer that pile was already six to seven feet tall, and we had broken up enough rock to plant corn. Uncle Dave had somebody bring some dirt in, and we planted corn and pigeon peas [*Cajanus cajan*]. There was this house in the middle of all this stuff growing around it. There was no grass and there were no flowers; everything was grown to eat. The next summer we came back and started chipping away at the front yard."

How can Williams explain the fact that the rock-breaking episodes didn't sour her on gardening? "Well, the thing was, what I remember is the eating, eating the corn and the pigeon peas and rice. Oh, how I love pigeon peas and rice with coconut milk," she said, describing the traditional Bahamian dish, which combines the flavors of onion, coconut milk, tomatoes, peppers, and spices with peas all mixed into the rice. "And some of that corn was popping corn. The cousins would hide at the back of the patch, build a fire, and pop some corn before Uncle Dave could find us."

Kenrie's front yard is small, but filled with plants—hostas and zinnias in the foreground, a grapevine along the fence, and potted annuals at the steps.

Kenrie advises gardeners to make good use of space by planting vegetables among the flowers. She's taken her own advice and placed the collards in the midst of impatiens and coleus.

56

By the time she was nine, Kenrie had her own garden. "We were living in Fort Lauderdale and my mom allowed me to have a five-foot-deep stretch of backyard," she recalled. "I remember my dad cleared out the sod and all that. At that time I didn't know anything about ameliorating the soil, so I planted whatever I could in the sandy ground.

"One of my aunts or uncles, Uncle Erroll, I believe, came over one day from the Bahamas with this small banana plant for me to try." Kenrie planted the tree and watched the first fruit begin to form, only to have the neighbor kids pull it off before it ripened. "I was so mad. I was so mad," she said, remembering the affront all over again.

Kenrie's solution, while effective, is probably not an option for most gardeners. "I had my uncle get me some chicken feet, bloody ones, and I tied them to my tree," she recalled. "All the neighbors thought we were crazy 'cause we were from the Bahamas. Then I started kind of chanting and dancing around the tree. I said loudly, 'If you ever touch my tree, you'll end up like these chicken feet.' Well, they never touched my tree again."

As an adult, Williams took a few years to find her way back to full-time gardening. She worked for a local community council, owned a crafting business, and ran her own lawn service. All the while she was growing vegetables for her husband and son. "I had to get used to Minnesota seasons," she pointed out, "because I'd been growing in tropical climates all of my life. Then I started trying to see how much I could grow in this five-by-thirty-foot bed and started canning the surplus. I liked doing it and we saved money."

Now gardening has moved into every part of her life. There's the home plot, of course. Because of her knowledge, friends often ask for help. She's designed and installed gardens for them. A few years back she started working for a local greenhouse as a florist and vegetable garden specialist.

"I try out new things and pass along better ways of growing vegetables," she said. "My newest experiment is with tomatoes. We don't have room for a separate compost pile at home. So I planted my tomatoes around chicken-wire compost towers. You just throw all your weeds and kitchen cuttings, like apple cores and corn husks, in the tower with a little soil. As it rains, the liquid compost is fed to the plants. My tomatoes look fantastic," she added, with a bit of triumph in her voice.

"Why do I garden?" she mused aloud, as though thinking about the question for the first time. "I garden because I like it—I like it. It's very comforting to me. I like sticking my hands in the dirt. And I like picking and pruning. I like it when people are amazed at all I raise. And most of all, I like watching it grow."

Clarence Krava

THE OLD-TIME WAY

In the fall, Clarence Krava always spreads a load of cow manure, "right from the cow barn." When the ground has warmed to seventy degrees in the spring, he distributes home-prepared compost around all the vegetables. For an extra shot of fertilizer, Krava pours on a "tea" made of fermented fish heads and remains. He raises most of his vegetables from seed and grows his own garlic, dill, mint, and oregano. If bugs threaten the crops, Krava mixes up a potion of detergent, beer, a few tablespoons of bleach or borax, a dash of whiskey, and water. "That'll usually take care of most bugs," he added, almost superfluously. Using a long weed folded in half, he splashes the mixture on his plants, "sort of like a priest sprinkling holy water," he explained. "You don't need a sprinkler. . . . That was the old time way at home, years ago," he added.

Clarence in the late 1930s atop the horse-drawn hay wagon with his father behind and his mother on the ground.

When Krava refers to the "old-time way," he means the practices his Czech parents and grandparents used on the farm near New Prague where he was raised. Because his mother became ill when he was nine, Clarence took on major responsibilities at an early age.

When he was a boy in the 1920s, nothing was mechanized, nothing was wasted, little was purchased. Farmers saved their seeds from year to year, they prolonged the season to make food last, and they canned the surplus to get through the winter. Their methods worked then, and they work for Clarence today.

Anyone who fears that a return to organic gardening means a drop in production should meet Krava. His gardens fill most of his needs for produce all year long—from the first fresh radish of spring to the winter-dug carrots. During the summer he feasts on an enormous variety—from apples to zucchini. There are pumpkins, potatoes, butternut squash ("it's not stringy"), sweet Spanish onions, and lots of garlic for the cold months. "Czechs love garlic," he explained. "The old-timers even rub a clove on their breakfast toast. At the early morning mass, you can smell that garlic all through the church."

To carry him through the winter, Clarence "puts up" pints of salsa and pickled beets, quarts of tomatoes, gallons of pickles and sauerkraut, jars of jam, and packages of frozen, homegrown corn. In addi-

tion, he has ample produce to give away. Lucky neighbors are the beneficiaries, as are the retirement homes in town. His children and grandchildren always get their supply.

Krava has large gardens because he enjoys the produce; he loves to cook and wants the fresh tastes his gardens provide. But his methods are lessons for the small gardener as well. He's great at stretching Minnesota's short season. By planting garlic sets and radish seeds in the fall, he gets a jump on spring. He'll put in several successions of cool-weather crops—lettuce, radishes, and members of the cabbage family—and he'll harvest broccoli and cabbage into November. "The cabbages don't freeze very easily," he said. "They can stand a lot of cold." In the fall, Clarence pots up his parsley plants and brings them indoors to grow on the windowsill. "That way I can pluck fresh leaves all winter. I don't use any of those onion and garlic powders in my cooking either, just the real stuff."

Krava has a unique way of storing cabbage. In harvesting the last mature heads, Clarence pulls them up, roots and all, and stores them in a basement refrigerator. "In the old

days, Mother put them in a root cellar, under straw," he said. By Christmas, his cabbages look gray and dry. "You'd think you'd better go to the store and buy one. But you pull off the two outer leaves,"

he said, "and they're as white as snow and taste fresh, because they get their moisture from the root."

Though Clarence has deep respect for the old ways, he's just as keen to try something new every year, as long as it fits into his philosophy of organic gardening. He's tested numerous varieties of tomatoes; one of his catalogs offers over four hundred. Recently he has come back to 'Big Boy' and 'Early Anna,' plus 'Roma.' A few years ago he started canning salsa, so now he's planting jalapeños, red peppers, and sweet banana peppers to give color and flavor to the mix. He has tried dozens of pickle recipes—sweet, dill, and sweet and sour. His latest innovation is a sun-processed pickle, which involves setting the jars on the driveway in the hot sun for days. It's not for the faint-hearted, but oh, so tasty.

One of Clarence's three gardens, this plot produces corn, beans, tomatoes, and onions. His bountiful harvest supplies friends and family, as well as meeting his own needs.

After seeing overpriced seed tapes in the catalogs, Clarence devised his own, using newspaper and a mixture of flour and water. He places the seeds evenly along strips of newspaper, covers them with the flour/water mix, and then lays the strips in rows in the garden. "The newspapers hold moisture and I get good germination that way," he said.

In the last few years he's had success digging in two tablespoons of Epsom salts around his peppers. Later when they bloom, he sprinkles an Epsom-salt solution over each plant. "I find that more blossoms set fruit with that treatment," he explained.

Clarence spends a lot of time on gardening—thinking and planning during the winter, planting and

61

Clarence uses lots of cabbages for his homemade sauerkraut and for eating fresh well into winter.

harvesting the other months. It's obvious he likes to get his mind around a topic and understand it thoroughly. "A lot of the fun of gardening is trying your hardest, having a failure, and then figuring out what went wrong," he said, with the chuckle of one who usually succeeds.

Krava exhibits the same skill and generous spirit in the kitchen that he does in his garden. He's a widower now, but has done the cooking for years. He cooked even while his wife was alive, because of her heart trouble and because he enjoys the process. "I love to try out recipes," he said, thumbing through a neat stack of gardening and housekeeping magazines. "I just started subscribing to a new magazine that has a lot of really good ones."

Clarence can describe intricate Czech delicacies like *jitrnice* (Czech sausage), which a friend helps him prepare twice a year. The elaborate production requires the rendering of pork necks and heads and the grinding of the everpresent onion and garlic. Bread is toasted and crumbled, barley is cooked, seasonings are added. The whole mixture is stuffed into casings. "You have to use the real casing, not the synthetic," he emphasizes, "then boil it for five minutes. You have to watch it carefully."

He makes preparing other Czech specialties—potato dumplings, poppy-seed kolacky, *zelnicky* (sauerkraut cookies)—seem as simple as toasting Pop-Tarts. But these treats are not for Krava alone. Every fall he cooks up a huge picnic for his whole neighborhood. People come and feast for hours. At Christmas his children and their families gather at his place for traditional rolls and kolacky, plus fresh vegetables, like kohlrabi and carrots just out of the garden. Often there's *buckta*, a braided sweet bread with prune filling. Krava can always find new reasons to celebrate—the wedding anniversary of young neighbors or the visit of an old friend. When he says, "I love to entertain," it seems like an understatement.

At seventy-seven, some folks might think of slowing down. Not Krava, who tells the visitor, "I'm hard to get. If you want to call me, try at about seven in the morning or six to seven at night. Otherwise, I'm usually out." Halfway into one gardening season, he's already thinking about additions for the next—an ornamental plant holder for the front yard and a new kind of bean to try.

Clarence finds satisfactions at every corner of his life, because he's doing what he loves. "I probably go out and just look at my garden nine, ten times a day. I like to see what's growing. What I enjoy most is the outcome. I was a stonemason for years and I enjoyed that you could stand back and see what you'd done. Gardening's the same. You put a seed in the ground and you get this fruit. It's an accomplishment."

Beatrice Garubanda

AN AFRICAN GARDEN

By the time children are two years old in Uganda, their basic toy is a hoe. "As you get older, they make the handle longer to accommodate you," recalled Beatrice Garubanda, in the melodious accents of her homeland. "By the time you are sixteen, you have your own patch of garden and can plant anything . . . anything. What you would like to eat and what you would like to see growing. Sometimes you would even find a patch that has a banana tree which would never go anywhere. As long as you like it, that's what you grow," she said, laughing softly at the memory.

Hearing Beatrice's remembrance, an American might picture a charming childhood diversion, but the subject is hard work. Children have their part to play in a culture where gardening is a full-time occupation. "Everyone in the village, everyone must participate," she said, referring to the rural area in western Uganda where she grew up, "because you are not just looking at raising a few vegetables, but at producing enough food for the whole family for the whole year. So if you planted carrots, it would be a big plot of carrots. If you planted onions, it would be a large plot.

"You had to be constantly vigilant, because there is no point in planting if you cannot harvest. So you had to wake up very early to protect your crops from animals and bugs."

Harvest, too, was hectic. The family, particularly the women, had to get crops dried and stored before rain came. "Basically the women do more of the gardening," Beatrice said, "because the men were always working with the animals, fencing them, and taking care of them.

"In Africa we dried. We did lots of drying. That's the way we preserved things. We put things out in the sun—beans, peanuts, all the

Beatrice and her children in her African garden. Front row: Esther and Joshua. Back row: Beatrice, Lydia in the baby-sitter's arms, and Beatrice's sister.

pulses. Then the grain is dried, the corn. We dry onions, too. They don't get completely dried, but that is the way you keep them from sprouting."

Vegetable gardens were close to the house because there was no refrigeration. "You had to pick your vegetables every day, so you had to have a garden where you can get things quickly," Beatrice said.

In Uganda's climate, crops grow year round. "There was no winter," she explained. "The only time it is too hot to grow anything is June, July, August. In most cases people would have looked ahead and planted crops that could be harvested then."

As Garubanda talked about her own youthful gardening, her three older children folded clothes and tended to two-year-old Umba, who wanted to climb in his mother's lap. "They were so young when we came," she said, "and they have no memories of anything. They don't know anything else except life here. They don't know anything about the garden."

Her children's experiences will never be the same involving agricultural life she knew, but Beatrice is teaching them her skills. "They help a little bit. They were trying to weed, but they are still clumsy," she said good-naturedly. Aware that they will never have to depend on what they grow for food, she presents garden work as an option, not a necessity.

Coming from an agricultural community like Uganda's, Beatrice minimizes her efforts here. "I don't want to arouse suspicions that I am doing some big job. This patch of land I garden," she said in amusement, pointing out the newly spaded earth behind her house, "wouldn't even be acknowledged in Uganda. Maybe they would say it was like a sixteen-year-old's patch."

Beatrice and her husband, Jim, have been in Minnesota for eleven years, since he came as a student. She has gardened the last eight. Because the Garubandas and their three small children were in an upstairs apartment at first, Beatrice sought out a community garden. Now that she has a yard of her own, she is finding spots to plant her favorite vegetables. A large shade tree and four active children mean that good gardening space is at a premium. "I'd rather have my kids playing basketball here, instead of always running to the community center, where I can't see what is happening," she said.

Garubanda's scattered plantings mean that she's growing fewer crops than in other years. "Last year in my community garden, I grew things I don't have room for here— beans, lots of them, and kale and collard greens and carrots," she said. "I had the Swiss chard. Swiss chard is one of the new vegetables in Uganda. People really like it because it comes back after you pick it. Also I had eggplant. I was able to freeze my collards and green onions. The tomatoes I froze lasted almost all the year."

Now, Beatrice plants the essentials, many of the same crops she had in Africa—white and red onions, cucumbers, broccoli, brussels sprouts. The Ugandan favorite, "walking" onion *(Allium cepa),* is there to provide green onions all summer. Beatrice has only two

Despite limited space, Beatrice has grown many of her favorite vegetables, including a healthy crop of cucumbers.

WALKING ONIONS
(*Allium cepa*, var. *proliferum*)

Walking onions, also called Egyptian onions, have been grown for centuries. These top-set onions are very hardy perennials that produce table-ready green onions during the plant's first year. The Egyptian onion is an odd-looking plant, forming a crown of small bulblets at the top of a two-to-three-foot tubular stem. As the weight of the topset increases, the bulblet falls and plants itself up to two feet away from the mother plant, hence the name *walking*. Because they are sturdy and prolific, walking onions are often passed from gardener to gardener.

Walking onions. Photograph by David Cavagnaro.

banana peppers ("I am not a spicy person," she explained), but lots of tomatoes, cherry and full size. She's growing cabbage, both short and long season, summer squash, and strawberries. She's trying "wild spinach" (amaranth). "It does very well in a place with a lot of humus," Beatrice explained. "The more you pluck it, the more it will produce. When it flowers, you can keep the seeds. My friend kept her seeds and gave them to me."

The size of Beatrice's current plot differs greatly from her African gardens, but her techniques are similar. "Basically, I use the same methods here as in Uganda," she said. "But here I have water. I had to wait for rain in Africa."

Garubanda spades over new ground to prepare the plot. "That's the only part of gardening I don't like, breaking the ground," she said. "I can weed, that's no problem, but I don't like starting. So I just turn over a few shovelfuls every morning. Here I reserve most of my peelings and vegetable cuttings and bury them in the garden. In Africa we had manure from the cattle and some of the humus from the coffee husks. Those are very helpful for

the soil. Also we would let a plot rest for a while, or if you planted beans one year, you wouldn't plant beans there the next."

Another difference Beatrice noticed was in her source of seeds. "We used to save seeds from everything, everything, even bananas," she said. "Actually, bananas produce a lot of younger ones. So you dig them out and transplant. But here you can't save seeds, because they don't come back the same way."

Most of her seeds come from the African stores in town. "I haven't asked for any seeds from home," Beatrice said. "Maybe I could, if I wanted to, but you can get almost everything in Minnesota." You can get the produce as well, she noted, but it is expensive.

Though her vegetables are ones she knew from Uganda, her methods of preparation have changed. "We have a tradition of steaming," she explained. "We put leaves at the base of the pot, and then put in banana leaves. We do a lot of banana leaves. We sauté some meat and wrap it. Then we wrap all the different vegetables and put them in the pot to steam. Within one hour, the food is ready, and you have

your starch, you have your meat, you have your vegetable."

Without readily available banana leaves, Beatrice does a lot of sautéing and boiling. "But I don't do much baking and making casseroles or whatever," she explained. "I put my foods in a pot and cook on the top of the stove."

With four children at home, including an active two-year-old, Beatrice has many claims on her time. Still, she prepared new ground and claimed all the sunny spots in her yard for vegetables. "We'll be eating fresh vegetables at a reasonable cost," she said. "Besides, it's something I like to do. I love most to see the plants grow. You know, from the seedling to the plants to the harvest is joyful, just like watching a baby grow. From the time I put in the seeds, that's my joy."

Austra Nora

Even at age eighty-one, Austra Nora remembers vividly the sights, scents, and tastes of her Latvian childhood: the fine meal made of fresh rye bread, a slice of smoked pork from the meat cellar, and the just-picked dill and onions. "*That* was a good sandwich," she recalled. When currants ripened, Austra was "like a little girl. Many times I disappeared into the currant bushes to eat. They were so sweet." In her yard there was a bush that was "very popular in the old country. It smells so good when you touch it, and usually when you cut flowers for the house, you always cut a couple branches."

Nora lived eighty miles east of the capital city of Riga, on a farm where "everything was made at home and everyone was busy every day." Her family grew vegetables for themselves and the animals. They raised barley for beer and berries for wine and jam. Austra and her brother gathered cran-

berries, mushrooms, and wild blueberries from the woods and fields. In the fall, the women harvested the apples and made sauce and cake. "See, we didn't buy apples," she said in explanation. "We tried to make them last until Christmas, or maybe January." They shredded cabbage for sauerkraut and prepared large barrels of pickles.

Using chamomile and mint and flowers from the meadows, her grandmother brewed medicinal teas in homemade cloth bags. "The grandma's job in the family was to care for people if someone was complaining about sore throat, or chest pains, or some other ailment," she said. "That would be my job now," she added laughingly.

The family prepared food for the animals, cooking up flour and potatoes for the pigs and chopping beets for the cows. "Now you can just go to the store and buy pellets," she noted.

The work was hard, but Austra's life was laced with pleasures. She recalled the "little tree that smells so nice. Those trees we connect with nightingales. When those trees were blooming, the nightingales are singing, and that is a kind of romance time for young folks," she recalled with a laugh.

Flowers were plentiful. "Latvians, they really were so much for the flowers," she said. "They spent lots of time on them. Of course, many girls had to take care of the flowers and weed them." Farms had U-shaped and circular beds filled with perennials and self-seeding annuals.

In the middle was the fragrant southernwood *(Artemisia abrotanum).* "Nobody in the spring just went to the nursery to buy anything," she said. "For our big district we had only one nursery and that was for apple trees and for the orchard." Instead, people collected seeds in the fall for spring use or relied on annuals to seed themselves. Austra remembers marigolds, snapdragons, cosmos, zinnias, and morning glories. There were sunflowers as well, but they differed from the ones she sees in Minnesota. Those in Latvia were not plants with one blossom, but mostly those with a hundred flowers on each plant. "Hollyhocks we had, too," she said. "In the fall they are really beautiful."

"Very popular" were many of the same perennials she's found here: sweet William, phlox, lupines, "lots of daisies, oh, we had lots of daisies," peonies, and roses. "But we didn't have fancy roses like you

Austra's colorful garden combines favorites from Latvia—phlox, irises, daisies, and hollyhocks. Her careful, but casual arrangement allows each plant to look its best.

have nowadays," she said. "We just had big, wonderful bushes. Jasmine [mock orange] and lilacs we had in the old country, too, lots of those."

Nora remembers even some of her chores with pleasure. Of mushroom hunting she recalled, "Wow, how I did enjoy that in the old country, to walk in the woods. I knew the places where every kind grew. Even in the evening when I went to bed and closed my eyes, I saw mushrooms, mushrooms."

After a childhood filled with rural pleasures, she excelled at school. When she and two girlfriends made a pact to study dentistry, "we were a group of three good friends and we all made a plan to study it," she laughed. "It was hard to get in, you know. I had to prepare myself. I was studying maybe fourteen hours a day for the whole summer."

Was it unusual for a girl to study dentistry in Latvia in the late 1930s? "Not exactly," Austra said, minimizing her own ability and initiative, "because Latvia at that time was a country mostly of farms, and we did not have too many big industries. So, many young folks went to our capital Riga and studied."

Corn was a new crop for Austra when she came to Minnesota. Now she considers it as essential as her beets and beans.

73

But World War II interfered with Austra's plans, and she was able to practice dentistry for only one year after completing university studies. With no trace of bitterness and not

The blossoms of pale yellow hollyhocks look especially delicate against this rugged wooden post.

a little humor, Austra recounted her own immigration story.

"Latvia was like a little country in a good position for the Germans and Russians," she explained. "They both try to get us. At one point the Germans kind of chased the Russians away, and then one year we had the Germans in and they took what they needed. Then Russia came and they took what they liked from Latvia, so they kind of destroyed the country completely.

"When the Russians came back later, we knew who they were. They took away every private farm, every private source. Nothing belongs to you anymore, and so we fled with the Germans to Germany. We were planning to get back sometime after World War II.

"But after the war somehow they divided the country so the Russians could stay in Latvia. We stayed in Germany until we had the chance to get to any other free country, like Australia or Canada. Some went to Sweden." In Germany, Austra met her husband. "We chose the States," she said. "I can say we made the right decision. We were really happy."

The Noras first came to North Dakota and worked for six months on a farm, but then moved to southeast Minneapolis for work and study. "I was planning to study in the university, but then I got my family," she said without regret, "and gave up my dentistry."

Thirty years later the family was joined by Austra's seventy-six-year-old mother, who had remained on the farm during Russian control. "She looked so old when she came," Austra said. "I thought she'd come to die." In the warmth of her family, she revived and lived twenty more years. "Granny was ninety-seven when she died," Austra said.

The Noras bought their country place after Granny came. "She was the one who took care of the garden then," said Austra. "She had chamomile and mint and the special teas. She felt like she was on the old farm again."

Nora herself maintains some of the old ways. She has a large vegetable garden and currant and raspberry bushes. From her apple trees she makes sauce and coffee cake; from the raspberries, jam. Many of her favorite flowers are around the yard: hollyhocks and sunflowers,

BIRDCHERRY AND SOUTHERNWOOD

"The little tree that smells so nice" was the European birdcherry *(Prunus padus),* similar to the chokecherry *(Prunus virginiana).* It is found in southern Canada and the New England states, as well as in Europe. A low, spreading tree, it can reach forty feet in height and bears pendant stalks of cup-shaped fragrant white flowers in April and May. The elliptic, dark green leaves turn red or yellow in autumn.

Southernwood *(Artemisia abrotanum),* indigenous to Spain and Italy, has finely divided, grayish-green leaves and a strongly aromatic fragrance. In earlier times, it was thought to ward off infection and was placed at the side of prisoners to protect them from jail fever. Women carried large bunches of southernwood to church in hopes that its keen scent might keep them awake during long services. The volatile essential oil is absinthol, which is said to repel bees and other insects. Accordingly, the French call the plant *garderobe,* as moths will not attack clothing among which it is laid.

myself in this country because I am not sure about all the mushrooms," she said. "And I don't enjoy going in the woods like I used to. Here there is poison ivy and wood ticks. We didn't have those. . . . It's so different now."

But despite strong, sweet memories of the "old country," Austra refuses to romanticize the past and proclaim its superiority to later years. The clichéd phrase, "Bloom where you are planted," could have been written to describe her: she seems to have flourished at every age.

lilacs and mock orange, phlox and daisies. There are always cut flowers on her table and potted plants on the sill.

Austra makes compost, saving all her eggshells and peelings in an old milk jar under the sink. Alternating layers of leaves, kitchen wastes, and good soil, she gets bushels of rich compost each year to apply around the raspberry bushes.

Still, things change because the cultures of the old country and the new are so different. Her Minnesota garden has a greater variety, for example. "In Latvia we had onions, of course, and carrots and potatoes, lots of cabbage, lettuce, cucumbers, beets, pumpkins, and dill—they *like* dill. I remember when they started to have tomatoes. That was something new. At first, we didn't like it so much, you know." Now in addition she grows Swiss chard, radishes, and corn, which Latvians considered animal food.

Perceptions change as well. The currants that were so sweet to Austra as a child no longer taste so good. The mushroom picking that was such a delight is now fraught with perils. "Even I don't trust

Tatyana Gendels

I COULDN'T GROW ROSES IN RUSSIA

Tatyana Gendels traveled with her husband, Boris, one hour by train, then continued on foot for forty minutes to get to her garden outside Leningrad. Often the Gendelses toted seedlings or fruit trees on their backs; always they took along food and water for the weekend. Coming back to the city, they carried their harvest: strawberries, currants, apples, potatoes, eggplants, tomatoes, herbs. "We had no car," Tatyana explained. "If we could not get a ride with friends, we had to carry, carry, carry.

"For a while some bus drivers decided to make money. But it was a catastrophe because there were never so many buses, and always too many people. You know, everyone wanted to get inside the bus, and they were carrying large metal backpacks, tools, and bushes."

Every weekend from spring through fall, the Gendelses made the one-hundred-and-fifty-mile trip from their small apartment to their country place, their dacha, outside Leningrad. "We bought our plot of ground and built our little country house ourselves," Tatyana said. "It was very difficult because there were no materials, no market, nothing. But we picked up scraps of wood and materials from different places and built our shelter."

In the early years, the 1980s, Tatyana's garden was mainly flowers. "We planted flowers, first of all, for our souls. Later, we added vegetables and fruits and it was very, very necessary for us. They helped us survive. Do you know what you can find in the stores in winter in Russia?" she asked, with no trace of bitterness. "You can buy potatoes, carrots, beets—beets are very common—cabbage, and sauerkraut, sometimes turnips. That's it. Nothing more."

Finding plants for the garden was difficult as well, she said, "because the market is not so big. It is an absolutely different culture, absolutely. In America it is a thriving business—people have money to spend. But in Russia there are no nurseries and little money. So we exchange cuttings with friends. It is our main source for plants."

Annuals, like sweet alyssum and petunias, are found primarily in public squares, "but commonly in private gardens we see perennials," Tatyana continued. "People like them because they are more economical. It is not necessary to restart them every year. They spread fast, and you can plan for all-seasons blooming. Seeds are available, but

DACHA

More than 30 percent of Russian families have dachas, which are little plots of ground with cabins. In cities the percentages are even higher, because these small plots were traditionally distributed by trade unions to their workers. The main purpose of the dacha is not rest, however, but to be a place to raise food crops. Here, Russians by the millions raise large quantities of produce to supplement the markets' meager offerings. The government estimates that 25 percent of all vegetables consumed in Russia are grown privately on family plots or at dachas. The actual amount is probably much greater.

Using every means possible to stretch the season (starting seedlings in apartment windows, making cold frames to ward off frost, and building greenhouses when possible), these determined gardeners harvest fresh produce from March through October. Fruit, which is rarely available at the grocer, is especially prized.

they are a problem because people have no space in their small apartments to start them."

As a botanist at the Komarov Botanical Institute, Tatyana was well situated to begin her country garden. "I asked people for help, and they brought me so many plants," she said. "My colleagues and my students gave me quite a few interesting perennials." At its largest, Tatyana's garden contained three hundred different perennials, as well as a large vegetable and fruit collection, herbs, and a small greenhouse.

"It was Zone 4, like here, so I grew everything possible," Tatyana said, naming several of her favorites: goatsbeard, Maltese cross, globeflower, geum, primrose, and bergenia. She rolled off their Latin names with the ease of the trained botanist she is: *Aruncus dioicus*, *Trollius chinensis*, *Lychnis chalcedonica*.

"We had apple trees, black and red currant bushes, and *Aronia melanocarpa*," she said. "That is a very nice blackberry and is good for jelly and wine. I had eight different varieties of strawberries, early, mid-season, and late. Then if the early

one was struck by frost, I still had the middle and late. And if we had a rainy summer and I lost my middle, then we could harvest the early and late. Russian strawberries are very different from American ones; they are juicy and sweet. The one in stores here resembles a turnip, firm and large," she said with a laugh.

Every spring the Gendelses set up a small plastic greenhouse in the country to hold seedlings they had started in Leningrad. "Our apartment was small, but I preferred to start my tomatoes, cucumbers, and other things inside in February. Later we took them to the greenhouse. Also sometimes for fun we grew watermelons, a special greenhouse variety, small, sweet, with absolutely black seeds." Fertilizer, she explained, was provided by her pet parrot. "It makes very strong, very good fertilizer," she said.

Her herbs were "just a common collection": tarragon, lemon balm, basil, lovage, mint, yarrow, sage. "Common," perhaps, but Tatyana's knowledge about their uses is anything but ordinary. In Russia, she studied their effects on people and other plants and gave lectures to teachers and postgraduate students on healing herbs. Given the name of any herb, Tatyana can discuss its beneficial qualities. "*Melissa officinalis*, lemon balm, is a very great plant, because it is the only plant to treat myocardia [heart disease] and migraine. Russian doctors use it." Of mullein, which is native to Europe and America, Tatyana remarked, "This plant is fantastic. With *nepeta* [catnip] it works against the potato disease, fusarium wilt. A scientist at my institute was doing research on that.

"What happened in the last fifty years is that people forgot many healing plants. It is important to keep this knowledge before the new generation. Russian people know a little bit more about biological methods, because we are a rather poor country when it comes to chemicals. So scientists started researching natural products, what's under our hands, and found we had plenty."

As Tatyana described her gardens, the forty-five African violets in her apartment, the fruits and vegetables grown at the country place, and her research at the Botanical Institute, she gave clear evidence of the pleasure she takes in growing things. Her

Tatyana has covered her fence and several house walls with ornamental vines—sweet peas, the annual 'Morning Star,' and this dramatic passionflower (Passiflora caerulea).

focus has been this intense since she was a girl.

"I have dreamed about plants since my childhood," she said. "From the age of ten, I was a botanist, because I participated in a special botanical club at my school. We had a very big room for botany with a small greenhouse. Maybe my teacher helped me develop along these lines, because she allowed me to do everything that I wanted once she saw I was interested. I started planting and transplanting. I could come any time I wanted.

"Still, I cannot explain my enthusiasm. No one in my family had ever been attracted to this subject. In my very small apartment I didn't have enough space for my plants. But all my life I kept them in spite of that. They are something I must have. Perhaps botany is close to my soul."

In Russia, Tatyana was unable to grow roses. Now she's enjoying collecting hardy shrub roses, including this prolific Canadian beauty, 'Winnipeg Parks.'

As highly educated scientists, Tatyana and Boris held positions of importance in Leningrad, but when conditions in Russia deteriorated, they made plans to emigrate to Minnesota with their grown daughter, Olga, and Tatyana's mother. They came in 1994, facing the difficulties of all new arrivals: employment, housing, and language.

No life-wrenching transition is easy, but with intelligence and resourcefulness, the Gendelses have made a place for themselves in St. Paul. The skills Boris developed in building his country place served him well in transforming a run-down bungalow into a home. Tatyana has found work in her field and has begun gardening again. With the same zest she must have exhibited in Leningrad, she delights in finding the uncommon, the rarely seen. In two years, she has filled the yard with bloom from spring through fall.

"Have you seen this cultivar?" she asked, calling attention to a small-leaved, tightly crinkled ajuga, 'Cristata.' Or, gesturing affectionately toward the bright orange flowers of a rampant vine at her back steps, she questioned, "What do you think of this 'Morning Star'? A friend gave me the start."

As she walked around a yard brimming with plants, Tatyana made connections between her Minnesota garden and her Russian one. "This trollius is a good bloomer," she said. "I had the same variety in Russia." She pulled aside the leaves of a small flower. "The geum we brought with us. My mother put a cutting on her breast."

"I couldn't grow roses in Russia," she said, pointing out the hardy bloomers she grows here: 'Sea Foam,' 'Prairie Harvest,' 'Mary Rose.' "I have many of the same perennials that I had in Russia. But here I fell in love with annuals, because there are so many available. So now my garden is a mixed annual/perennial garden."

Since vegetables are readily available in Minnesota, the Gendelses no longer raise staples. But Tatyana continues to grow tomatoes ("that cherry is my husband's favorite"), several fruits (strawberries, raspberries, and currants), and the culinary herbs: basil, chives, parsley, mint. Her medicinal plants are there as well—borage, comfrey, lemon balm, lovage, mint, and sage. Just as in Russia, her indoor garden is thriving, and includes a few African violets that made the trip with her. "I talk to my plants, you know," she said, which may explain their healthy condition. She has passed on her love of gardens to Olga, who has designed several gardens since she came to Minnesota.

What are the satisfactions of working in the garden? It depends on the mood, Tatyana emphasized. "Sometimes we just like the physical procedures, digging and trimming," she said. "Sometimes we enjoy planning the landscape. Although for a real plant lover, the design is dynamic, because we are always bringing in new plants. And there is joy in going to the market and finding something new; this is our sophistication."

"Oh, you don't know how much I love this garden," she said, gesturing widely to include all her plants. "It is my soul."

THE TASTE OF HOME

Simeon Okwulehie

GROWING PEPPERS, GROWING HOME

he only pepper I grow that's not hot is the Hungarian wax," said Simeon Okwulehie, pointing to the rows of peppers in his backyard. "See, what I use peppers for, they have to be fiery." The varieties Simeon plants are definitely ones with bite: the red cayenne, the jalapeño, the Anaheim chili, the Thai, and the habañero (one of the fieriest around). Even the Hungarian wax, which Simeon calls mild, is generally known as a hot pepper. "When you grow up like I did with everything hot, you prefer it," he said in the cadences of his Nigerian homeland.

Simeon uses these peppers and the other African vegetables he grows for his consuming interest: cooking. He's famous in the local Nigerian community for pepper sauce and pepper soup, auctioning off jars of the sauce at the annual Igbo Fest celebration of Nigerian Igbo culture. He likes to prepare African specialties for his wife,

Diane, and their children. "I look at cooking as something I enjoy, not as a chore, so I like to take my time," he enthused, explaining the daily production in the kitchen.

Simeon learned his cooking and gardening skills at his mother's side, but acknowledged that few Nigerian men do either one. "In the typical Nigerian household, the man never gets close to the kitchen," he said with a laugh. "I know my father never did. But for some reason I always liked it. I kind of grew up in the kitchen. It got to the point that my mother would actually say, 'Go do the cooking,' even while my sisters were there." Now Nigerian women here seek out his recipes. "They tease me about my cooking, but actually they also ask for advice," he said.

Although noted for his abilities in the kitchen, Okwulehie is diffident about his skill, offering his recipe as only one of many ways to prepare a

dish. "Pepper soup," he admitted, "sounds like it's just cooked with peppers, but it's not. Of course, if you don't put enough peppers in, the eaters will say, 'What's this—meat soup?'"

In his soup pot, Simeon uses goat meat. ("We Nigerians like the older ones," he says, implying that the aging animal is an acquired taste.) In addition, he throws in some dried fish, three or four different spices (*uziza* and *uda*), Maggi, the peppers, and salt. "It's one of the dishes you make when you're having company coming," he explained.

Simeon grows several kinds of peppers for cooking and for his famed pepper sauce. These mildly hot Hungarian wax peppers add sweetness.

he raises vegetables familiar to Nigerians but exotic to most Minnesotans. "I grow the okra, of course, but I've come to prefer the spineless variety," he said, referring to the tiny prickles along the vegetable's skin. "Typically Nigerians, even the ones who live here, want okra with spines. But now I find that texture interferes with the taste. We Nigerians don't fry okra like they do in New Orleans. We dice it and put it in soup."

Looking much like a sprawling watermelon plant with speckled leaves, the *ugbogoro (Telfairia occidentalis)* takes up almost as much room as the peppers. "We harvest the leaves all summer, for soup," Simeon said. "Late in the season we can eat the fruit, shaped like the buttercup squash. A combination that is really good is the diced okra, chopped *ugbogoro* leaves, some crayfish, and a little meat."

On this mid-July evening, the *anara*, or garden eggs *(Solanum incanum)*, are just beginning to set fruit. But by late summer Simeon will have plenty for eating raw. The leaves can be eaten like spinach, and served raw or cooked. He's

With his cooking, Simeon can express his natural hospitality, sharing with friends the results of his work. In fact, his favorite recipe, pepper sauce, is made specifically to enhance the Nigerian custom of welcoming the visitor. "In our culture, we greet our guests by breaking the kola nut and offering it to them," he said. "We serve it at weddings and baptisms. Actually, any important event will include the kola nut. Pepper sauce is made as a dip for the nut. It's extremely hot."

Simeon's dishes are also a concrete way to pass on his heritage to his daughter, Chinyere, (meaning "God's gift") and son, Enyinnaya ("father's friend"). "You can learn the culture by eating the food and knowing what it is like," he observed. "I'm trying to get them prepared for when we travel to Nigeria. We want them to know a little bit of where they are from."

The garden, like the cooking, connects Simeon and his family with his home country, for here growing curry plant *(Helichrysum angustifolium)* and basil for his soups and is trying the tropical bitter leaf *(Vernonia amygdalina)*. "Oooh yes, this came all the way from Nigeria by way of Dallas. We're going to pile leaves around it come fall and hope we can get it through the winter." Bitter leaf is tasty in salads and soups, but is also good for stomach problems, Simeon said. The Okwulehies grow quantities of tomatoes, 'Roma,' 'Big Boy,' and beefsteak, which he and Diane will make into paste and can. "We don't have to buy any tomatoes all winter," added Diane.

And then there are the peppers. Most Minnesotans would recognize the plants, but few would grow the quantity and varieties in this garden. Simeon raises them all, because each pepper, though hot, has subtle nuances of flavor. The yellow Hungarian wax adds sweetness. The cayenne is mellow and sweet at first, hot later. And the habañero can set the palate wildly on fire. Simeon combines them all in his pepper sauce, that dangerous combination of peppers, spices, and fish that is cooked to a paste and then canned in great quantities.

IGBO VEGETABLE
(Telfairia occidentalis)

Telfairia occidentalis is one of the most important leaf vegetables of the Igbos of Nigeria, Simeon's group; in fact, it is sometimes called the "Igbo vegetable." Evidence pieced together from crop geography, oral history, and folklore, along with the intensity of its use, indicates that the crop is indigenous to Nigeria and has been cultivated by the Igbo people for centuries. It is grown wherever Igbos settle, but is rarely found in other areas. Because of its long association with the Igbo, *Telfairia* has become part of the language and the stories of the area. One proverb reads, "You are tender and fragile as a *Telfairia* vine tip."

The leaves are relished as pot herbs, and the oil-rich seeds are a source of unsaturated oils and proteins. The leaves and young shoots are first harvested for food after a month, and later every two to four weeks. These cuttings are cut or shredded and included in soups along with dried fish, peppers, palm oil, and ground seeds of the egusi melon. *Telfairia* is a fair source of protein and a rich source of iron and is administered as a blood tonic to convalescent people. Mature fruits provide seeds for planting, for flavoring soups, and for snacking.

Telfairia occidentalis

Though his garden has expanded and contracted over the years, depending on how much land has been available, Simeon has had one all his adult life. "I came to study at Mankato State in 1982," he explained, "because my sister was already there and because Nigeria doesn't have enough colleges for its high school graduates. So, of course, I didn't garden then. But as soon as Diane and I married and got our first apartment, we had a garden."

In years when he could garden on his in-laws' property in Gaylord, Simeon grew even more. Often he's planted *egusi*, or bitter apple *(Citrullus colocynthis)*, another watermelon look-alike and Nigerian favorite. Some years he's had black-eyed peas, and amaranth, a good green for stew and soup. Once he tried yams, but found that a Minnesota summer is too short to produce the large Nigerian tuber.

"Everyone had a garden in my country," Simeon said. "And all the children helped. You didn't really have a choice—your mother would say it's your turn." When he was young, the family lived in Lagos, the country's capital, because his father was employed there.

Today Simeon prefers the smooth texture of spineless okra over the varieties he knew in Nigeria. This short-season variety goes in many of his stews and soups.

In Nigeria, hibiscus grew freely near Simeon's house. He's found a Minnesota-hardy hibiscus to remind him of those Nigerian blossoms.

out and grab what you need and cook it—a chicken, a goat, some vegetables. It's all fresh. But here, since we have winter, you have to store foods for the cold months. Once I saw that, I said, 'Wow, you actually *can* food.' Now Diane and I can my pepper sauce and tomatoes and I enjoy it."

Despite the labor of gardening, or perhaps because of it, Simeon finds the satisfactions are many. "It's a way of teaching the kids about nature, and hopefully, they'll remember and say, 'My parents did this. They loved flowers and vegetables.' Maybe by the time they're ready to move on, they'll get into it, too.

"For me, it's an escape from the world. You get so tied into it, you forget other things. I guess I grow these things to keep from getting homesick. And then you actually start harvesting and you see the fruit of your labors. With this you feel, 'I have achieved something.'"

"My mother had a garden right outside and I just picked it up by watching what she did," he said. "Now I use a tiller to turn under my leaves, but otherwise I garden pretty much as I would in Nigeria. It's mostly organic farming there, and I stay away from chemicals, too.

"Actually, what I've been doing here is when the leaves drop, I pile them on the garden and put up a chicken-wire fence around. Then I keep turning them before it freezes. In the spring I do the same thing. When I'm ready to till, I take off the fence, and turn under what's left. It's pretty much all compost by then."

There is one major difference between Minnesota and Nigeria that Simeon has come to enjoy: canning. "See, the thing about that is, we don't believe in preserving food," he explained. "You just go

Ana Maria Saquiy Davis

I LIKE TO MAKE MY OWN GARDEN

ou know," Ana Maria Saquiy Davis said firmly, "women in Guatemala don't make the garden, just the men. The women keep the house, care for the kids. My head is different. I like to make my own decisions. I like to make my own garden."

On a small tree farm near Hewitt, Ana is doing just that. The weather, the vegetation, and the terrain could scarcely be more unlike her home in Guatemala City. Still, since 1980, a year after she married Peace Corps volunteer Dave Davis, this central Minnesota farm has been home, the place where the Davises are raising their boys. Her country was beautiful, she said, "everything is green." But there was no peace. "The men just gunned people down like chickens," she explained. In Minnesota, she and Dave can make a good life for their family. "Now," she said, "I am happy. I am a happy woman."

Because gardening is the job of men in her country, growing vege-

tables is a fairly recent avocation for Ana. But she had observed well and knew what she wanted to grow. Here, Dave has helped her get started. "Oh, my husband is a good man. He shows me what to do," she said.

Novice gardener or not, Ana has learned to deal with Minnesota's short, cool season and raises many of the vegetables she knew at home. As she walked around her twenty-five-by-fifteen-foot plot, Ana noted that gardens in Guatemala are much bigger than hers. "I don't have anything that special," she said modestly, listing more than a dozen crops she grows. There are green beans, onions, summer squash, and lettuce, all on gently mounded ridges just as in Guatemala. Neat bushes of zucchini and broccoli, plots of Swiss chard and spinach fill in the long rows. Ana raises plenty of tomatoes, for eating fresh and for freezing. She has tomatillos,

Ana and her husband, Dave, met and married in the mid-1970s when he was a Peace Corps volunteer in San Lucas, Guatemala. Photograph courtesy of Ana Saquiy Davis.

corn, and kohlrabi, and sunflowers and raspberries grow along the edge. There are several herbs: cilantro, thyme, and two kinds of mint, or *yerba buena* in Spanish, one for chicken soup and one for *chili dulce*, "sweet chile." Ana had oregano for a while, but it died one winter.

Of course, there are peppers ("I really like them," she said in explanation). This summer she's trying four, each with its own pungency—the banana, the jalapeño,

the *diente perro* ("dog's tooth"), and the serrano ("given to me by a friend"). Ana uses them for many dishes, but especially for *escaveche,* her pepper sauce.

Each cook has a recipe for this sauce, but Ana makes hers by frying the chilies, then adding cut green beans, onions, and a little garlic. She tosses in some *vinagre* (vinegar), "but not too much," and some tomatoes. The completed dish is, she said, "just yummy, yummy."

Everything here is grown without chemicals. To maintain fertility, the Davises spade in homegrown compost, made from weeds and kitchen waste. "I don't like to pour poison on my vegetables," she said. "My husband doesn't like it either. So we don't use chemicals for the garden, and we don't use them on the trees." Dave and the three boys still at home raise five different clones of poplars, which they sell for reforestation.

Ana has tried growing several other vegetables she knew in Guatemala, with no success. She's put in yucca two times, but the plant didn't make it. "It's just like a potato, and tastes very good," she said. "Maybe it's too hot, too cold, I don't know." Another summer she planted the bushy herb *chipilín*, grown for its leaves, which are "so good for you." But that didn't come back either.

She'd like to grow *güisquil* or *chayote* squash *(Sechium edule),* which in Guatemala is a rampant vine. Its pear-shaped fruit is good in soups and for stuffing turkey. But chayote squash grows in the tropics and can't survive in Minnesota. "It's so different here," Ana

Ana kneads the masa *for homemade tortillas.*

observed, echoing the sentiments of many who arrive from warm climates.

To supplement what she cultivates, Ana gathers two plants from the wild. "You call them weeds," she said, "because they grow up between the rows of corn." She collects pigweed *(Amaranthus retroflexus)* and a member of the nightshade family, *yerba mora (Solanum nigrum)*. Amaranth, a good spinach substitute, has a long and distinguished history as a food crop, wild and cultivated, and has been eaten in various forms by people all around the globe.

Yerba mora has an ancient history as well, but a more controversial one, and Dave worries when she eats it. Because of the active poison solanine, the nightshade family has long been considered harmful; it can affect the central nervous system and the gastrointestinal tract. Animals seem to avoid the plants unless there is no other food available. Still, groups in Asia, Africa, and the Americas have eaten it for centuries. Scientists wonder if the quantity of solanine varies at different seasons, if the method of preparation removes some of it, or if

Using a traditional stone (piedra de moler) *and rolling pin* (brazo), *Ana rolls out the dough.*

certain groups have developed an immunity.

Ana's decision is based on experience: she's always eaten it and sees no ill effects. "I eat a lot of leafy greens," she said. "I cook it a little time on the stove and add tomato

sauce and hot stuff. Oh, my goodness, that's yum, yum."

Ana's garden and the plants she gathers are important, because she is an accomplished traditional cook. The Davises don't make a run for fast food at night. Instead they sit

AMARANTH
(Amaranthus)

Forty-five species of amaranth *(Amaranthus)* are native to Mesoamerica, and ten other species have originated in Africa, Asia, and Europe. Several were important food crops among the Aztecs and earlier cultures in Central America. Because the indigenous people used the plant for effigies as well as for food, the Spaniards outlawed amaranth production. From that point, many species native to the area almost disappeared.

The amaranth family includes plants as diverse as tumbleweed *(Amaranthus albus)*, love-lies-a-bleeding *(Amaranthus caudatus)*, and pigweed *(Amaranthus retroflexus)*. On farms, the introduced varieties, like pigweed, are considered noxious weeds when they appear in the fields. High in calcium, protein, and iron, the grain is now used in cereals and bread. Gluten-free, it is useful for people allergic to gluten.

Amaranth. Photograph by David Cavagnaro.

down to one of Ana's homemade meals: tamales, tortillas, and chiles rellenos, but also soups and beans that she has seasoned and cooked. Until recently she ground and processed the corn for her own tortillas. Now she has simplified her life a bit, making the tortillas from scratch with *masa*, ground cornmeal.

The garden is important for another reason, Dave said. "It gives Ana a tie with her country when she can grow the vegetables she had in Guatemala. And it gives her a feeling of independence, as well," he said.

The difficulties of living in a new land can sometimes weigh on Ana. She struggles with the language and misses friends left behind. "I try to talk English," she said, "but it's so hard. I watch television and listen to the radio, and now I try to talk. But sometimes I feel sorry for the people listening to me," she said with a laugh.

Making friends helps the loneliness. "You know, you come into this country. You are alone. It's just good for you to have a friend. Now I have friends from Costa Rica, Salvador, Peru."

Ana's tortillas and other Guatemalan specialties are daily fare in the Davis household.

Despite the hard changes, Ana is a strong woman—she made the decision for her children. "Now my kids can have a better life," she said. "They are good kids."

Seeing things growing eases her mind. "You know, sometimes I think, why am I in this country? Then I go outside. I look at the trees. I look at my garden. Then I think, it's good to live in Minnesota. It makes me so happy."

Jerry Piazza

THE SICILIAN KITCHEN GARDEN

hough his garden doesn't have the fig tree or grape arbors his grandfather's would have had, Jerry Piazza's lush vegetable plot and small orchard are a fitting testament to his Sicilian heritage. Long rows of tomatoes and peppers, beans, winter squash, and Italian parsley flourish behind his Golden Valley restaurant, the Piazza Ristorante. 'Black Beauty' eggplants grow alongside a Sicilian variety called 'Mesanissi,' which Piazza raises from seed sent by his Italian cousins.

A Sicilian bush basil forms small, green mounds along the rows. "This has a much better flavor than what's usually grown here," Piazza explains, plucking off leaves. Cucumbers, chard ("Italians use a lot of it"), zucchini, and *Cucuzzi lungo (Lagenaria siceraria)*, a narrow, Sicilian, hanging zucchini-like gourd complete the eight-by-ninety-foot garden.

Jerry [on the left] and his family by the grape arbors. Photograph courtesy of Jerry Piazza.

In a grassy strip along the street, Jerry tends five apple trees ('Sweet Sixteen' and 'Haralson'), four Parker pears, and a Toka plum, all producing fruit. "These don't do as well as I'd like," he said, "because there's too much wind blowing off

97

Medicine Lake and too few bees to pollinate."

Piazza grows the vegetables for his restaurant's salads, stuffed peppers, minestrone, and sauces. "Our customers can always tell when we're using fresh produce," he said. But as he walks along the immaculate rows, pointing out varieties and checking on problems, it's clear he grows these beauties for the pleasure of gardening as well. "I learned this all from my grandpa," said Jerry. "He was a great gardener."

Jerry's grandfather, Agostino Piazza, was his teacher and mentor. Coming in 1892 to Morgan Avenue in north Minneapolis, Jerry's *paparanni* brought the strong gardening traditions of his native Termini Imerese, Sicily. "Our family has been farming on the same land since about 1840," Jerry explained. "There are still cousins there."

The elder Piazza had intended to come to America, make a good income, and then return for the family. "But he didn't like the boat," said Jerry Piazza, "so he stayed and sent for his wife and children." Jerry's father and grandmother arrived in 1899.

In Minneapolis, Paparanni raised vegetables to feed his family and to sell around the city. "He had about three city lots full of vegetables," said Jerry, "over five hundred tomato plants, plus lots of green and Hungarian peppers, zucchini, carrots, and beets. In July he'd start endive, which lasted into November. Everything was grown just so—no weeds and in straight rows." There were no ornamentals, explained Jerry, because his grandpa always said, "You can't eat flowers."

"Every day he'd hitch his horse and wagon, fill it with the produce, and drive all the way to Prospect Park," said Jerry. "He'd leave early and wouldn't get home until eight o'clock at night. It was a hard life."

Piazza remembers grape arbors that ran along the sidewalk and between his and Paparanni's houses. The families grew Concords for jelly. "My grandpa really knew how to grow grapes," Jerry said. In the fall the Piazzas bought quantities of zinfandel and muscat grapes from California to make wine, between 125 and 150 gallons.

Only one crop gave Paparanni trouble—the fig. "Italians have a great affection for figs," explained Jerry. "They [his grandparents] grew a large fig tree in a pot and would bring it in every winter. They'd ooh and aah when they got even a few fruits."

Now, Jerry Piazza is continuing the family gardening tradition. He's gardened all his life, and for nine years he's maintained the restaurant's large vegetable plot. It's an unlikely spot—in the middle of a commercial development. All around are parking lots and office buildings. But Piazza makes it work with a combination of love and solid technique.

The addition of leaves and fertilizer (20-10-10) every year has made the soil soft and fertile. "People bring me their leaves in the fall," he explained. "I leave them in the bags until spring when I spread them out, put the fertilizer on top, and till it all in."

Piazza buys many of his seeds commercially and is always on the lookout for new varieties. This year he's trying a lemon cucumber,

The Italian eggplant "Mesanissi" is a favorite of Piazza's for its "meaty" taste and tender flesh.

Irene Loudas

A GREEK GOURMET

eople catch their breath when they see Irene Loudas's garden, and well they might. Its size alone (about one hundred feet by sixty feet) is impressive. "Everybody asks me who helps with this plot," she said. Except for occasional assistance from her husband, Basil, this is Irene's responsibility. "Sometimes I spend the whole day weeding, from eight o'clock until dark," she said.

"She gets lost in there," Basil added, pointing to the long rows, "and I wonder where she is. Then once in a while she stands up, I see her, and down she goes again."

More noteworthy than the garden's size are its contents. This is a diverse garden, supplying the ingredients for the sophisticated Greek food Irene prepares daily for family and friends. An innovative cook, she learned many techniques from her mother ("most Greek mothers are good cooks") and from Greek cookbooks, but she is not afraid to experiment. Her dishes call for fresh herbs and vegetables that are often unavailable at the market.

Like her cooking, Irene's gardening is experimental and adventurous. Irene doesn't simply grow eggplant, for example; she has three varieties, including a Japanese one. These go into the Greek national dish, moussaka, as well as other Greek specialties: eggplant salad, sautés, sweet preserves, and pickles ("eggplant is my favorite pickle"). She raises three types of potatoes and four kinds of onions, as well as okra, beets, garlic, broccoli, and leeks, which are important in northern Greek cooking.

Loudas has numerous fruits—raspberries, apples, grapes, plums, strawberries—good for eating fresh and for marmalades and jellies. The mint, thyme, chives, dill, oregano, celery, and parsley she grows add pungency to her meals.

Anyone who believes that the tomato is a round, red fruit should look to Irene's garden, where yellow, oblong, pear-shaped, and multicolored tomatoes thrive. She savors the subtle differences each one adds to her recipes. "The yellow is high in vitamin A and is sweeter," she said. "The Greek tomato is good for salads."

Loudas grows several peppers, sweet and hot. "I have yellow and orange and a sweet red one called 'Florina,' a city in Greece," she said. "We like to roast peppers and stuff them with rice, meat, herbs, whatever. In October I make a pepper sauce which is typical of northern Greece, where I am from.

It calls for hot peppers, like jalapeños, and sweet peppers that have turned red. It is very, very tasty. When I'm making it, the whole house smells wonderfully peppery."

Swiss chard, cabbage, grape leaves, and even zucchini blossoms are grown as wrappers for filling. "Greeks do a lot of stuffing," said Irene in amusement. "Stuffed zucchini flowers are a special delicacy," she said, and a delicate operation as well.

To ensure a steady supply, Irene plants a zucchini called 'Sunburst,' which is not only beautiful, but produces many male flowers. "I pick the blossoms every morning and refrigerate them so they won't close up," she said. "After I've collected enough, I fill them with rice and seasonings, close the tops, and place them in a casserole with egg/lemon sauce, then steam the whole thing. The blossoms give the dish a subtle flavor."

Irene and her family came to Minnesota when she was fifteen, she said, because "times were diffi-

cult then in Greece. I am from the northwest corner of the country, from a town called Kastoría, near Albania and the former Yugoslavia. I was born high up in the mountains where everything was green, with snow in the wintertime and lots of rain in the spring. It is not unlike here, but is very unlike the rocky, southern part of Greece most people know.

"The landscape was beautiful, and I loved being outdoors. I remember those growing-up years as a very happy time, and the garden was a part of that. My grandmother used to sit there stringing beans and cooking zucchini. I thought it was just the greatest thing."

As a young wife in Minnesota, Irene found it difficult to buy the herbs and vegetables for Greek dishes. "Now there's such variety in the groceries," she said. "But do you remember when the only vegetables you could find were potatoes, carrots, and onions? There was just one lettuce, iceberg, and

Irene raises many herbs, but basil is of singular importance, for its religious symbolism and for its culinary uses. Here, basil flourishes amid the marigolds, dill, and eggplant.

105

Irene raises okra for several Greek dishes, and enjoys its beauty as well. She noted that the blossoms are as lovely as a small orchid.

the only spinach was frozen. That's what got me started, I think."

Gardening has been a consuming passion ever since, even when she had a full-time job. "It was hard, but I did it. There are so many satisfactions and the food is so great. You know, Greeks use a *lot* of vegetables and a little bit of meat.

We're talking about the Mediterranean diet."

Despite the greater variety available now, Loudas continues to grow vegetables for their freshness and because her own produce is organic. In addition, she still raises crops rarely found at market: French dandelions ("they have bigger leaves than the wild variety"), purslane, amaranth, and stinging nettle. "They are so tasty and very good for you," she said. "You look forward to different produce at different times of the year. Early spring you associate with dandelions, because they are one of the first things up."

She gathers greens from the wilds as well. "I get so excited in the spring," she enthused. "I go foraging for different plants, because it's so much fun. It is traditional where I am from. These greens are very nutritious. I read that if you eat nettles every day, you don't have to eat anything else because they are just packed with all the nutrients. And lamb's-quarters, that is a lovely thing, very delicious and mild. We use it as a substitute for spinach."

"In fact," added Basil, "they have just discovered that purslane is

very good for your heart. It has the omega-3 that you find in fish oil."

Many of Irene's crops have special significance, either because of their use in favorite dishes or because of their ties to home. However, sweet basil is of singular importance, and she grows five varieties.

"Basil means *royal*," she explained, "and has religious significance for us. When Saint Helen, mother of Constantine the First, uncovered the cross three centuries after Christ's death, she found basil growing there. So, there's no Greek that won't have basil growing in a pot or in the garden. We distribute it at church on special holidays. The priest uses it in blessings. And of course, we put it in much of our food. It is grown for its fragrance also."

Irene is self-taught in gardening, and obviously well taught. She has a large collection of books, magazines, and catalogs and can discuss varieties, growing techniques, and soil preparation with the ease of a horticulturist. She starts many of the plants—the tomatoes, peppers, leeks—from seed to get an early jump on summer. "This year we had tomatoes by the Fourth of

PURSLANE
(*Portulaca oleracea*)

Purslane *(Portulaca oleracea)*, though often considered a weed when found in American lawns, is a very popular vegetable in other countries. It has been used as a food for so long that by 1535 there were three hybrid varieties available in seed catalogs. It was introduced in Massachusetts from Europe as early as 1672 and is now a recurring weed everywhere. The tips, gathered young, before flower buds appear, are like New Zealand spinach and can be eaten as a salad green or in soups. The stems make a succulent pickle.

In the garden, purslane spreads over the soil surface, making a living mulch. A tough plant and hardy to Zone 3, a small portion of the fleshy stems will take root under adverse conditions. Because the stems and leaves store water, purslane survives during droughts and even when hoed out of the ground and left on the soil surface.

Recently scientists have discovered that purslane is filled with omega-3 fatty acids, which are effective at fighting cholesterol. It is also rich in iron and vitamin C. In China, the whole plant is given to reduce fevers, and the juices are used to treat skin diseases.

July," she said. To further stretch the season, she plants cool-weather crops like cabbage and broccoli "as soon as the ground can be worked. Here we have sandy soil, so I'm out there shortly after the snow is gone. You know, if you don't plant peas in March or early April, you can just as well forget about them."

Though having wonderful produce is clearly important, Loudas spends so much time in her garden because she loves the process. "You take the garden away from her," interjected Basil, "and it's going to be real bad."

"Working out there brings many satisfactions," said Irene. "Maybe only other gardeners can understand. But there's so much beauty—even the leaves have interesting shapes and lovely colors. The flower of the okra, for instance, looks like a little orchid, off-white with a yellow center.

"You feel good when you're outside. Your mind clears. If you have a problem, you can sit and stew about it or you can go out in the garden and relax. Things just kind of take care of themselves. It's good to be close to the soil. It's a spiritual thing, a very spiritual thing."

In late summer Irene's sunflowers tower over most vegetables. The blossoms look dramatic in her fall bouquets, and the seeds feed the birds.

Enrique and Zenaida Zavala

A MEAL FROM MICHOACÁN

ast year it was better," said Enrique Zavala, with the typical modesty and high standards of gardeners everywhere. "It's not good this year for growing the plants. I don't know if it's Mother Nature or what." Despite his disclaimer, on this late June day Enrique was already harvesting cucumbers and zucchini and his cilantro was about to go to seed.

The season had been a strange one, a warm spring followed by cool temperatures and rain in June. So Zavala's tomatoes and chili peppers were not as far along as usual. Though his production wasn't as plentiful as he had hoped, the vegetables were tasty. "I don't put any fertilizer or anything on them, just water," he said. "I don't put anything in my garden but the shovel. I think when you do, you can taste the chemicals."

Enrique has been growing in Owatonna for two seasons. "Even when I lived in the camps [the migrant worker camps] I had a garden. I grew cabbages and pumpkins, chilies and everything like here." Now with a house and a yard, he's putting down more permanent roots. Not only does he have vegetables, he's planted grapes that will need a few years to begin bearing well. "Last year I had so many cucumbers that we used all we could and then I gave them away to friends. The tomatoes were this high," he said, holding his hand three feet above the ground.

Enrique's garden is there to provide the ingredients for his wife Zenaida's masterful cooking. In her hands, a few zucchini, onions, tomatoes, cilantro, and cumin become a delectable dish. With tortillas and cheese, she has produced a meal for her family of five. "One of her specialties is *corundas*, or tamales," Enrique said. "These are not the usual tamales. She makes them with corn leaves, the green ones. They taste different, wonderful. They are a specialty of our region of Mexico, Michoacán."

Zenaida's *corundas* require a whole afternoon of preparation, but are well worth the effort. Enrique harvests and softens the corn leaves; Zenaida prepares the tamale dough. Everybody helps stuff and wrap the leaves. After steaming, the tamales have absorbed a fresh "corny" taste from the leaves.

"All the Mexican people use tomatoes, chilies, onion, garlic, because it tastes so good," Enrique said. Not surprisingly, he is growing these same vegetables, plus squash,

cucumbers, strawberries, and sunflowers. He grows three varieties of chilies—serranos, jalapeños, and banana peppers. The fiery serranos and jalapeños go in salsa and stir-fry; Zenaida stuffs the banana peppers with cheese. "All the time people say that those Mexicans take a lot of chilies," said Enrique. "We do, but chilies don't just taste good, they are good for you, too."

Cilantro adds its distinctive flavor to many traditional dishes. "When you make a chili, it tastes better if you use the green leaves of cilantro, rather than the dried," Enrique said. "The cilantro is in almost all the food we eat. In fact, cilantro is so popular in Mexico that one factory makes a candy for Christmas with a cilantro seed in the middle. You are waiting for that taste when you bite into it." The Zavalas allow their cilantro plants to go to seed, then Zenaida dries the seeds and saves them for next year's crops.

Enrique grows three kinds of peppers for Zenaida's dishes. Here, jalapeños are ready for cooking. Photograph by David Cavagnaro.

In addition to the vegetables they grow, the Zavalas gather two greens, *verdolago* (purslane or *Portulaca oleracea*) and *quelite* (lamb's-quarters, or *Chenopodium album*) for use in salads and sautés. Both are very popular staples of Mexican cooking and are sold in the open markets there. "This one is everywhere," Enrique said, picking up leaves of the lamb's-quarters on the edge of his lawn.

Zenaida recommends sautéing the greens with onions and tomatoes. "You can add pork meat to the *quelite*," Enrique said. "You cook *verdolago* and *quelite* the same way, but they taste different." Purslane has a bite and lamb's-quarters tastes more like spinach.

"Many people don't like these greens just because they haven't eaten them before. These people say 'I don't like it' before they even taste them. But they have vitamins. They taste good." Enrique is right; lamb's-quarters is a powerhouse of vitamins A and C and one of the healthiest vegetables around. Purslane is an effective cholesterol

Corundas, *a specialty of the Zavalas' home region in Mexico, are tamales wrapped in fresh corn leaves and steamed.*

fighter and contains almost as much iron as parsley.

The Zavalas both are knowledgeable about medicinal plants. *La mansania*, chamomile, helps soothe an upset stomachache, Zenaida said. *La menta*, also known as *yerba buena* (mint), is good in cooking, and also settles the stomach. To calm the nerves and clear the blood, Enrique recommended a tea of linden flowers. "You need to wait until the flower has opened up before you gather it," he advised. "In Mexico people come from all over to gather the blossoms. There are many, many things you can eat which will help you."

Enrique learned about gardening as he grew up in west-central Mexico, in Michoacán, "halfway between Guadalajara and Mexico City, only four hours to each. That's where I lived. It's beautiful because there are a lot of lakes, rivers, and mountains, beautiful mountains. The part where I lived they have many, many different kinds of fruits and vegetables, lots of roses, everything, everything. And all the time it's not hot, not cold. All the time it's warm, and it's green all year long.

LAMB'S-QUARTERS
(*Chenopodium album*)

A very old vegetable in northern Europe, lamb's-quarters (*Chenopodium album*) was probably introduced by the Romans in areas where their legions were stationed. Once regarded as the most delicious of vegetables, it lost favor when spinach was introduced from Asia in the sixteenth century. The name is a corruption of "Lammas quarter," a harvest festival held August 1 in the ninth-century English church. Brought to this country by the early European settlers, the plant has naturalized throughout the United States and is found along roadsides and waste areas.

An easily grown perennial, the plant contains more iron, protein, vitamin B2, and vitamin C than cabbage or spinach; its leaves make excellent greens. They are also used in herbal medicines. The women in some Amazon tribes eat the plant to encourage breast milk. Mexicans use the leaf to treat asthma, calling the plant *Herba Sancti Maria*. The plant's main use was to expel intestinal worms from humans and animals; all parts contain a worm-repelling compound called ascaridole.

Lamb's-quarters. Photograph by David Cavagnaro.

"We had avocados and corn and strawberries in every season. There were mangoes and bananas and guavas. In Mexico I had maybe four, maybe five guava trees. In the U.S. they are so expensive to buy in the store. And avocados you can buy here at two dollars apiece, but in Mexico you can buy one kilo, which is about two pounds and something, for one peso—one peso.

"We grew many of the same vegetables in Michoacán—corn, tomatoes, squash, chilies, green beans. But the plots are so much bigger. You could put this yard only for corn or squash," he said indicating his deep town lot. "Another place you could grow only beans.

"I learned as a kid, you know. My grandpa told me that, and my dad told me other things, and my mom told me, too. Down in Mexico most people had parents who could teach them about gardening, because everybody had a garden."

As busy as Enrique is, working long hours at the canning factory, he finds time to work in his garden. "Whenever I have time, all the time, I go to the garden, and it makes me feel better," he said. "All your problems are gone because you don't think of anything else when you're out there, just the plants."

Enrique says he's lucky to have Zenaida help out with caring for the vegetables. "Just men garden in Mexico," he explained. "Sometimes women help. It just depends on the kind of person she is or maybe the kind of person you are. But all the time Zenaida helps me. She pulls the weeds out and helps me plant. She likes many gardens, whether they're flowers or vegetables, just as I do."

Gardening is a good hobby, Enrique explained, because it is relaxing and because he wants the fresh food. "I like it," he exclaimed. "I really like it. When you go to the stores, they don't have that many things from Mexico. And when you grow it here, it's more tender."

Insom and Boun Saeng SouVandy

LAOS ON THE PRAIRIE

he sky is big in Pipestone, the earth is flat, rainfall is sparse, and trees are few and far between. The climate and terrain differ radically from northern Laos, where Boun Saeng (Boon Sang) SouVandy's family grew guavas, coconuts, and tangerines around the house. But after ten years in four different refugee camps in Thailand, the SouVandys and their relatives are grateful to be in Minnesota, even if it is a world away from their large rice farm.

Life was hard in Thailand, explained Boun Saeng without complaint. "We couldn't garden," he said. "We did grow vegetables at the first camp, but at the others the rules were very restrictive, so they didn't allow people to have a garden." He spoke carefully, describing the world so distant from the small, tidy apartment he shares with his parents. As he talked, his mother, On, played quietly on the floor with her granddaughter Tia.

Food was given by a United States relief agency. "They brought food for us, about one kilogram of sticky rice per day for each person, and about three ounces of chicken or two ounces of beef. Then we also got some vegetables like beans or pumpkins," SouVandy said, remembering the simple fare.

Boun Saeng couldn't garden, but he spent his time productively, learning languages in preparation for a future in another country. Still a teen when he entered the camps, SouVandy studied Japanese and French, and most importantly, considering his final destination, English. "Oh, I learned English in 1978 in the first refugee camp, with a Hmong teacher. The Hmong are the Laotian mountain people," he explained. "My family are Lao, from Sayaburi province in the north.

"I studied about three months and then went to study with a British teacher from England, Janet Becker. With her, I got better English. After I studied about seven months, I went to buy a book of grammar and started to look words up in the dictionary. Soon after that I began to teach English to pupils in the refugee camp and taught six hours a day," he said, demonstrating once again that the best way to learn a subject is to teach it. Today he continues to help his parents study the language. "We study and read books in the winter," he said.

In a country with no winter, only a dry season, Boun Saeng helped his father, Insom, with the farm. It was a large place where they grew rice "for the sticky rice [the staple food of Laotians]. We used buffalo to plow the field. We grew all our own vegetables, peanuts, onions, watermelons, cilantro, hot Thai peppers, and cucumbers."

"Cucumber we can eat three ways," he said with a smile, knowing that most Minnesotans serve it raw. "We can cut it into pieces, put it in the stir-fry, steam it, or eat it with the hot pepper sauce and sticky rice."

"Hot pepper sauce and sticky rice are the top things," he said, proceeding to describe the favorite

foods of Laotians. "We bake the pepper or cook it on top of the stove to make it soft. Then we peel it and cut it into small pieces and put it in a mortar and pestle," he said, demonstrating the grinding motion. "We add some cilantro, some garlic, some onion, and some salt and mix it. It is really hot. Then we put it in a bowl and eat it with the sticky rice [rice rolled into balls for dipping]. My mother makes a big pot of sticky rice and we eat it for every meal."

Also on his farm were lemon and orange trees, palms, grapefruits,

limes, and guavas. "We grew those in the yard. We miss those, too," he said, recalling the pleasure of fresh fruit and tall trees. "Also we grew bamboo, sweet bamboo [sugarcane] around the house. When the shoots came out, we could eat them. Sometimes we steamed them or put them in soup."

When Boun Saeng was a young boy, this lush scene was a giant playground, as well as a place to work. But life changed for him when he was eleven. "In Laos, I used to help my father when I was eight years of age until I was eleven. Then after that I could not walk," he said simply. "On the way to the farm I was running and I fell down and at the night I was very, very hurt and I could not walk again."

Boun Saeng's fall was his second serious accident. At age eight he had slipped into a quagmire and had had trouble getting out. He injured his knee and it became badly infected. Though the infection eventually subsided, the knee was permanently weakened. Three years later, when he slid down a slippery slope into a rice paddy, both legs were seriously hurt, and infection set in once more.

The SouVandys raise dill and cilantro for spices, mustard for stir-fries, and miniature corn for eating and for use as a thickening agent.

"In the small countryside where we lived, there were no doctors, no hospitals," he said. "It was a very uncomfortable time for me. After that, I stayed at home all the time and I crawled around the house." Boun Saeng and his family assumed he would never walk again.

With the loving effort that only a parent can muster, Insom SouVandy carried his son out of the country five years later, promising the Communist authorities that he would bring the boy back. "In 1976 [when Boun Saeng was sixteen], my father carried me from Laos to Thailand to live with my aunt, who had found a traditional healer to help with my legs. The healer massaged my legs with powdered sesame oil and a kind of herb—I cannot remember what they called that herb. After one month's treatment I could stand up and then I could walk with two canes. After three months I could walk with one cane. After six months I walked without using any canes," said Boun Saeng, remembering the details with the sense of wonder he must have felt at the time. Today he can walk and drive a car, but he still feels discomfort, especially in cold weather.

The family had promised the authorities that Boun Saeng would come back, but in fact they were all planning to escape. In 1978, they began to travel at night, hiding during the day. Because the guards were usually less observant after two in the morning, the SouVandys traveled then. They survived on the sticky rice they had brought. It was a difficult time for them, said Boun Saeng quietly, describing an experience that must have been extremely frightening, but they all arrived safely in Thailand and began their long wait to come to America.

Finally, in February 1988, under sponsorship of the Iowa Refugee Service, the SouVandys came to Sioux City, Iowa. They moved to Pipestone in April of that year. In 1995 Boun Saeng and his two brothers became citizens; their parents passed the test in 1998.

Here, Boun Saeng and his family can garden again. The Pipestone Seventh-Day Adventist Church they attend has made a large plot available to them. Though the climate precludes guavas and citrus fruits, the essential Laotian vegetables are thriving. "We grow some onion, garlic, hot Thai pepper, cilantro,"

BITTER MELON
(Momordica charantia)

Bitter melon *(Momordica charantia)*, a member of the gourd family and thus a relative of squash and cucumber, has been cultivated in Asia for many centuries. It has been known in Europe since at least the late seventeenth century, when it was illustrated in a Dutch garden treatise. Resembling a long, bumpy cucumber, it appears often in Asian and East Indian cooking. Its slightly sour flavor becomes quite bitter upon ripening, due to the alkaloid morodicine. The long-stalked, yellow flowers are vanilla-scented in the morning.

It is widely used as a medicinal plant in Asia to treat colds, flu, fever, colic, hepatitis, and stomachache. In China, doctors use it for diabetes mellitus, a use supported by studies in Sri Lanka (the plant contains a substance similar in effect to insulin). The vine tips are an excellent source of vitamin A, and a fair source of protein, thiamin, and vitamin C.

Though a world apart from his Laotian farm, Boun Saeng's Pipestone garden has the essential crops—long rows of multiplier onions and cilantro and smaller amounts of beans, bitter melon, and mustard greens.

Boun Saeng said, taking a mental inventory of his plants, "dill, lemongrass *[Cymbopogon citratus]*, gourd, pumpkin, bitter melon squash *[Momordica charantia]*, beans, mustard greens, and a small corn."

As he walked around his large, well-tended garden, Boun Saeng described favorite dishes and methods of preparation. "Lemongrass, cilantro, and dill are the basic seasonings," he said. "We add dill to fish soup to make it smell good and taste good. Lemongrass also gives flavoring. We mostly use the leaf in soup and the bottom part in stir-fry. It gives a good taste to the walleye, catfish, and crappie that my father catches in South Dakota."

Most of the Laotian vegetables are familiar, but the varieties used and the great space allotted to particular vegetables are a surprise. There are rows and rows of garlic and multiplier onions *(Allium cepa, aggregatum)*, those interesting plants that increase in a tight circle around the original bulb. Lovely in bloom, great quantities of cilantro border the garden. Smaller patches of corn and squash are at the corners.

Boun Saeng pointed out uses for the vegetables unknown to most Minnesotans. "We eat the ears of corn, of course, but we also crush the leaf into bamboo-shoot soup," he explained. "It makes the soup thick like Jell-O. And when the pumpkin plant is young, we steam the leaves and eat them with the pepper sauce. When chopped into small pieces, the bird-house gourd is an ingredient in fish or chicken soup." The SouVandys dry seeds and onion sets in the fall and save them in bags until the following spring.

The SouVandys save money with their garden, explained Boun Saeng, because now they don't have to go so often to the Asian store in Worthington. Besides, their home-grown produce tastes fresher. "Gardening is something like a hobby for us," he said. "We like to take out the weeds and grass, and we like to water. When we are at the garden, it reminds us of our home in our country."

LESSONS OF THE GARDEN

Seitu Jones

COLLARDS AND COMMUNITY

or Seitu Jones, gardening is not simply a hobby or a diversion, like cards or tennis. Rather, Seitu sees himself in a long line of black gardeners reaching back to his great-grandfather, a slave who fought in the Civil War and then came up-river to farm. The line includes his farmer grandfather; an uncle who gardened in St. Louis; his father and aunt, who grew vegetables and flowers in the Twin Cities; and "all the marvelous, unsung black folks who've been gardening for years."

It's a humbling legacy for Jones, who modestly insists he's just a "novice gardener. I really don't know anything." Seitu credits his forebears, whose stories and examples paved the way for his own gardening experience. "They all liked to be outside, and they all liked tending the garden," he explained.

These role models have left their imprint. Despite his modesty, Seitu is a skilled and passionate gardener

who has raised vegetables and flowers most of his adult life. Currently, his personal gardens in the Frog-town neighborhood of St. Paul include "one that's completely decorative and is all native plants." There he's planted a sustainable landscape that includes shrub roses, asters, the delicate fronds of little blue stem grass, coneflowers, and a huge stand of Joe-Pye weed, all framed by a handsome wrought-iron fence.

"Well, it's low maintenance," Jones said of this garden. "That's one reason I used native plants. This part of St. Paul was never prairie; it was wetlands with creeks running through it. But by putting in prairie plants, we can at least remember what covered so much of Minnesota."

His other home plot is "all food—a kitchen garden," he said. "It's all food we eat or give away. We like to cook and to give a lot of

Seitu, two and a half, in front of his grandfather's garden at 914 Fuller Street in Minneapolis. Photograph courtesy of Seitu Jones.

123

the produce away to family and friends." Seitu has experimented over the years with various crops. Now he's raising broccoli and basil, lots of tomatoes and collards, plus golden raspberries and plums. Sunflowers the size of small trees feed the birds; bee balm attracts butterflies.

Seitu's personal gardens satisfy on many levels. "I like being outside," he said. "It's something I can do in the yard with the grandkids. I got them some little gloves. My granddaughter likes to help. My grandson doesn't really like to work, but he likes to be outside.

"I like watching the plants grow and I am amazed at the scale of it, these little bitty plants that get so large. I like eating the stuff that comes fresh from our plots. And gardening's helped bring me back to health after my heart attack. I don't have any way to quantify that," he said with a chuckle, "but I feel like it has done that."

Seitu's home plots are personally gratifying, but the community gardening may be even more important to him. Deeply committed to Frogtown, Jones sees his efforts as a way of revitalizing the old neigh-

borhood and changing its public image. It's a large goal, but the last few years he and others have accomplished a great deal.

"I started working here first with Public Art St. Paul in the nineties, just as an artist looking at public art opportunities," he explained. "One of the issues that kept coming up was the number of vacant lots, about sixty lots scattered over fifty-some odd blocks.

"Housing here is about one hundred years old, and it was all worker housing, inexpensive housing. There was always a high percentage of rental property. The lots are small and many have two houses on them. What would happen is an immigrant family would come in, build a little house in back. Then when they got enough money, they would build another house in the front and rent out the back or send for other relatives. So these houses were never put up with any great care.

"The lots are only about thirty feet wide, some are twenty. Since city codes now require five thousand square feet to put up a house, no one could build a new house when the old one came down. People didn't know what to do with

Striking against the wrought-iron fence, these prairie plantings of grasses and flowers make a low-maintenance border and remind Seitu of Minnesota's earlier days.

Seitu's handsome stand of collards framed by taller cannas demonstrates that food plants can be as ornamental as flowers.

the lots. Again and again in these meetings the idea of green space or pocket parks kept coming up. So we set about doing that, and we've done about six of them as demonstration sites for quiet meditation; they were too small for playgrounds.

"Working with the Urban Lands program of the Sustainable Resources Center [a group working to foster community garden efforts] and with money from a wide range of sources, we did these little sites to show people how to create sustainable landscaping. They're something to see—one little garden the kids even came up with the name [Blazing Star Garden]. We put two benches in there and a little plaza

made up of old recycled sidewalk blocks. We've used native plantings for shade and sun. There are three kinds of asters, rough and medium blazing stars [liatris], wild geranium, and wild ginger—twenty-two kinds of perennials altogether. Now people just kind of sit up there quietly."

Making great use of neighborhood "muscle," Jones has secured grant money to hire young people to weed, plant, and lay paths. Men in the Four Seasons, an employment program of the Thomas-Dale Block Club, help prepare and maintain the sites. "These guys shovel sidewalks and mow lawns, handle small demolition and construction projects," said Seitu. "It's fantastic. Every year

they acquire more equipment, so now they've got a bobcat and a bunch of lawn mowers."

The parks have been immensely successful, Seitu said. "First of all, people use them—that's the bottom line. People said they would be vandalized, that people would pull stuff up or steal vegetables sitting there, and some of that has occurred, no question about it, but not in any kind of amount that would anger or even discourage us. People have taken on these parks with a sense of ownership."

In addition to the pocket parks, Jones has helped organize the Frogtown Farm, a 122-by-125-foot piece of land in the neighborhood. Here thirty-one different Frogtown residents are growing crops for family use. "Frogtown is St. Paul's most diverse neighborhood and it is reflected in the gardens," Seitu said. "Many yards are too small for vegetables, so people are excited to have some land available." Here, styles and crops run the gamut from plots laid out in tidy rows bordered by marigolds and petunias, to plots where corn, squash, and mustard greens are intercropped. There are gardens of herbs and flowers—

lemon balm, parsley, scented geraniums, gladioli, and nasturtiums—and gardens with hot peppers alone.

Frogtown has always had gardeners, Jones emphasized. "But these visible projects have encouraged folks to the point where we formed a quasi-garden club. And in 1998 we had our first annual garden tour. We wanted to change the perception people have of Frogtown.

"Sure enough, people came to the tour from Minnetonka, Mound, and White Bear. We heard comments like 'Wow, I never knew there were so many nice houses in Frogtown, so many nice gardens in Frogtown, and even so many nice *people* in Frogtown.'"

Seitu's plans for the future include more green space. "We want to create a working farm on scattered sites here in District Seven and District Eight," he said. "This would be a farm that would actually generate income. I'd like to see it concentrate on cooking greens. I'd also like to do an orchard with a wide range of fruits and that could be part of the farm. We could sell to local restaurants or even door-to-door.

"Now in most neighborhoods there is no nearby source of fresh,

quality produce. Everyday I see this army of people pass under my window heading for the bus, and I see them returning later with their bags. I'd like to see a return to the old days, when a bicycle cart went around selling produce."

In thinking about his work with public gardening, Jones has come to realize that a role model was at work there, just as in his home gardens. "If there is anybody I want to give some credit to outside of my family, it's Maurice Carlton," he emphasized. "He was a community gardener before anybody called it that. He carved out these little vacant lots and tranformed them into gardens. The biggest one was at Selby-Dale.

"He always wore red, black, and green, which we in the sixties thought we invented as Black Liberation colors. Come to find out, those were the official colors of Marcus Garvey's Universal Negro Improvement Association [UNIA] of the 1920s. This self-help, self-empowerment group was created in Harlem and really spread across the country. So Maurice was a part of that.

"Maurice had worked on the railroad as a sleeping-car porter and

settled in St. Paul when he retired. I met him when he was at the Inner City Youth League. He would go up and down alleys rescuing old dolls, tennis rackets, and broken TV sets and transform these things into little mixed-media sculptures. Now we call it outsider art, folk art, naive art. Lot of people laughed at him and called him crazy. He called himself a toy inventor, and I saw the work out of the corner of my eye all those years.

"Just recently I saw his pieces again at the Historical Society, and I was struck by its impact on me. Maurice was a part of that generation of black men who had stable, middle-class lives and cared for their families. He was a member of the UNIA and was using their colors as he carried on this work in the community. I had always thought that I was a part of that legacy. After thinking back on him and what I am doing, I see that this really is a path I am emulating. I'm trying to make this a more livable community for the people who are here."

Kevin Oshima

THE BONSAI MASTER

Kevin Oshima remembers clearly his first task when studying bonsai in Japan. "The master came out and handed me a straw, a shaft of wild grass, about this long," Kevin said, holding his hands twelve inches apart. "'Go collect these, all the same,' he told me." When Kevin asked how many to gather, the master simply said, "Collect them, no questions."

On Oshima's first try, he brought in straws of somewhat differing sizes and was sent out again with the directive, "All the same."

"So I went out and collected all day from morning till night, a whole pile of them," Kevin said. The next day the master showed Oshima how to make a broom and left him with instructions to sweep the temple steps. Kevin's job was to sweep from top to bottom, top to bottom, continually. "This went on for days," he remembered, "up and down until the broom was worn

out. And then I was sent out to gather more straws and start the whole thing over."

It was, he recalled, a difficult routine for an American kid, not really used to that kind of discipline. "We got up at dawn with the big bell—BONG. Up immediately, we ran down to the freezing river, threw water on our faces, brushed our teeth, and rushed to the temple ready to meditate. That was my exposure to the true Japanese style," he said.

The lessons were difficult, but from his tasks Kevin learned patience, and from the schedule, discipline. Even today he has incorporated practices learned in Japan into his life. He's up with the sun and ready to go to work. In the summer his staff arrives at 4:45 A.M., and by 5:00 "everybody is at their task."

Kevin Oshima, a third-generation Japanese American, is a bonsai

expert, one of the last of the kind. He learned his art from the eighty- and ninety-year old *senseis* in Japan. Though not technically a "master," which, as he explained, is a "revered title given to people who have studied for years," Kevin is clearly a highly skilled practitioner. His artful miniatures, row upon row of small trees, stand as serene testaments to his ability.

Bonsai is his occupation and his passion. He gives instruction, nurtures new and growing trees, and cares for the trees of his clients. "I just fell in love with bonsai," he said, slightly amazed at the fact after all these years. "For me it was the perfect combination of science [horticulture] and sculptural art."

It was also a way to bring more Japanese culture into his life. "As a kid growing up in Edina, how many Asian kids do you think I knew?" he asked. "Nobody in my family speaks Japanese. We are the third generation away from Japan. I always wished I had more Japanese culture in my life."

Kevin first saw a few bonsai trees at his grandfather's house and became intrigued. "It got hold of me," is his explanation. But there was no support from his family, who wondered about the financial wisdom of the choice. Still, once Oshima had decided, he was not to be dissuaded. And after a degree in horticulture and time spent collecting plants, primarily in the rain forest, he went to Japan to study.

Rather than study only under one master, as is usually done, Kevin opted to move from *sensei* to *sensei*. "Particular schools specialize in particular trees," he explained. "So a master becomes an expert in maples, or holly. I wanted to learn them all, so I had each *sensei* refer me to the next. I wanted to study

with all the old eighty- to ninety-year old *senseis* that I knew would be leaving soon."

Oshima absorbed the lessons well and teaches as he was taught. "The information that is given must be passed on," he said. "My obligation is to teach until the day I die and to teach the exact techniques that were taught to me. I don't alter them at all. That's very important because it makes a direct statement on preserving a cultural art in the pure sense of the word. In Japan there are fewer and fewer bonsai masters. When I go out, I want to be the last *sensei*."

Oshima runs the business in traditional ways. There are no computers, and personal contact with the client is paramount. A large part of his business is caring for his clients' trees during the winter. "They must have cold temperatures, high humidity, and high light," he emphasized. "If any one of these factors is missing, the tree will not make a proper rest. Most firms

Massed together in his yard, Oshima's specimens show the variety and subtle beauty of bonsai plantings.

make their clients sign a waiver, saying that the firm is not responsible if the plant dies." Kevin guarantees that he will replace any bonsai that fails under his care.

Oshima's tools and supplies come from Japan, as does much of the soil and the trays in which the plants grow. The trees, too, are primarily heirs of trees from the Japanese Imperial Collection. Some, like the apples or hollies, were grown from seeds Kevin collected there. Others, such as the maple, were rooted from cuttings gathered when the Imperial trees were pruned.

New workers begin just as Oshima did in Japan, not by gathering straws, but by performing other simple, repetitive tasks. Frequently they wash his car or mow the lawn until they are ready for a more difficult job.

These practices would be merely interesting if Oshima's bonsai pieces were not such fine examples of the art. The essence of bonsai is not

A moss-covered floor and the staggered placement of these small trees demonstrate how bonsai plantings replicate grander landscapes.

simply a little plant. Rather, it is a very small tree with the appearance and spirit of a real tree. The plant and its setting—that is, the container, the moss, the gravel—must be in balance in form and color.

First and foremost, the practitioner needs to see the possibilities of the tree. "Maybe the tree is too thick, or maybe it's bent in the opposite direction," Kevin said. "That's when the real inspiration comes in, when you are able to use what exists and make it more pleasing to the eye."

The work is tedious and precise. Trees need to be wired and trimmed, watered and root-pruned. They must be repotted and the soil improved. If a branch gets broken, a new one is grafted on. These tasks must be performed day after day. The care of the tree extends over years, for a truly distinguished tree does not come quickly.

The result, when all goes well, is a work of art. "You don't have to be any kind of art critic or any artist at all, you don't even have to be sighted to enjoy my work," Oshima explained. "You can touch it and those who can can look at it. The trees will speak for themselves.

Wrapping plants with wire is one method of shaping, as shown in this Japanese red maple.

The tree says, 'Here I am, I am a little Japanese tree. I look just like a big tree, and I'm just as old or older.' Every one of my pieces is very Japanese, in that the simplicity is the point."

In a world that asks for instant satisfaction, the appeal of becoming a bonsai expert may be limited.

But for Kevin it is the lifestyle that "made the most sense. You do what you want to do, but you also have a certain presence of discipline about you. I can't wait to wake up in the morning."

Maiju Köntii

SMUGGLED ROSES

Flying home from her sister's house abroad a few years ago, Maiju (Mayu) Köntii carried rose cuttings in her purse. "My three smuggled roses," she called them, two old-fashioned varieties and her favorite, 'Midsummer's Night,' a white shrub rose that blooms in late June. The small cuttings have become robust bushes, filling her St. Paul yard with flowers and fragrance, and reminding her of home. "That white rose is absolutely the one. I can't imagine having a garden without it," she enthused. "In Finland it blooms at the peak of summer during our biggest holiday, *Juhannus*, Midsummer Fest."

Grounded for the winter, Maiju served coffee cake in the spare elegance of her living room and talked with characteristic intensity about her favorite avocation. "The 'Midsummer's Night' rose bloomed by my girlfriend's sauna," she recalled. "They are at home in

country places. And when my sister moved to Sweden, I took it as a present to her." After starting her own garden here, Maiju made cuttings once again. "It makes you feel good to see it—you say 'I always had it.'"

Köntii can't remember when she started gardening, but thinks she has done it "more or less all [her] life. Everybody has a big garden in Finland," she said. "All the people in the countryside grow their own vegetables and fruits. And they all have perennial borders. My father died when I was five, so we moved in with my grandparents. They had a huge amount of apples and berries. There, we always had a long perennial bed. My grandfather had planted it just so, with tall phlox, all different colors, in the back and small astilbes in front. Of course, we had spirea in the yard always, so that's one of the things you want."

A young Maiju in her Finnish garden. Photograph courtesy of Maiju Köntii.

Maiju loves the look and fragrance of old-fashioned roses. The alba here, 'Königin von Dänemark' (Queen of Denmark), has elegant blossoms and a heavenly scent.

Maiju remembers in vivid detail the rhythm of chores at her grandparents' place, where the apples and berries were grown for the market as well as for home use. "It was like a job," she explained. "In the morning you just went to the berry bushes. My sister and I got paid for helping. First, you went to the currants, red and then the black and white. Then you went to the gooseberries." Every liter she collected earned her fifty pennies. "We marked each bucket down in a little book," she remembered.

When the cabbages got wormy, she and her sister picked them off by hand. "Our grandfather used to pay us by the piece," she recalled with a laugh. "We had to bring the worms to him. Bribery works well with children."

Perhaps most intensely she remembers the sensuous joys of being outside in a short summer. To her, the phlox, which in Finland bloom late in the season, have an "end-of-the-summer smell, like dark August nights." The best berries were always the black currants, "which have a most delicate flavor. You can't get them over here," she said, "but when eaten with raspberries, they are really a nice treat." Good weather was to be savored. "There are not so many nice days over there, so you just put your

Against her tall hedge, Maiju has placed a blend of pastels—peonies, irises, and roses. The hedge gives her privacy and provides a solid backdrop for the flowers.

ESPALIER

According to the *Oxford English Dictionary*, the word *espalier* comes from the Italian word *spalliera*, meaning "wainscot work to lean the shoulder against." In espalier, fruit trees are dwarfed and trained to grow against the shoulder or wall of the garden. The technique first became popular in the walled medieval gardens of Europe, where space was limited. One of the earliest depictions of espalier dates from the fifteenth century, when a detailed French/Flemish painting shows a wall with espaliered fruit.

By training the trees along the walls, gardeners could grow them with relatively little growing room. They soon found a second benefit: the warmth from the stone or brick wall helped the plant to leaf out early and the fruit to ripen more quickly. Third, the open pruning allowed light to reach all parts of the tree. Not only were harvests bountiful, but the espaliered tree was an elegant addition to the garden.

Favorite trees to train include apple, peach, plum, cherries, and pear. They may take any number of forms, including the fan, the candelabra, and the cordon (a simple horizontal arrangement).

food on the tray and ate outside. Or you would have the late afternoon coffee in the garden. Even now, it can never get too hot for me because of those cool summers."

To compensate for long winters, Finns have lush indoor plant collections, Maiju said. "All our windows have very deep sills," she said, "to accommodate lots of plants. People grow any kind of houseplant there, not just beautiful things."

Horticulture brought Maiju to Minnesota as an exchange student in the early 1970s. She worked for a local nursery, propagating the seasonal flowers, Easter lilies, roses, and mums. When the year was up, she returned to Finland, but traveled back and forth to Minnesota for several years.

Returning for good in 1975, Köntii began a seven-year association with Bailey's Nursery in Bayport, one of the largest wholesalers in the country. There she did all the manual labor connected with a commercial operation. Her litany of the work is reminiscent of the time at her grandfather's. "First I worked in the propagation," she recounted, "and then many summers I was trimming mugho pines,

you know, down on your knees. In the fall, there was the tipping. In winter, the grading. It was really hard work." Maiju no longer works in the fields; for years now she has managed a friend's catering company. "Still to this day," she said, "I think of the workers and wonder how they are doing when it rains and the weather is bad."

All the while Maiju had her own gardens, first in south Minneapolis and now in St. Paul. She chose the St. Paul bungalow because of the oak with its low-hanging branch out front, the birch tree in the back, and the mix of pale fuschia phlox and rhubarb at the garage. Soon enough, she began altering the landscape. "The first year I planted a hedge," she related. "Yards are really private in Finland. Even very big yards in the countryside will have a hedge around them. I keep mine tall, but skinny, because my yard is small."

Then Maiju added some of her favorite plants: spirea, hydrangea, and lily of the valley. "I have lots of lily of the valley in little spots around the yard. That absolutely is a Finnish thing for me," she said. Besides the three smuggled roses,

The strong vertical structures in Maiju's garden—Japanese tree lilac, a wooden trellis, and a tall green hedge—frame her colorful plants. The cascading 'William Baffin' rose, creamy 'Madame Hardy,' and delicate coral bells add a riot of color and shape.

northern European design; everything extraneous is removed and all that remains is beautiful and functional. The walks are edged, the tomatoes staked, the hedges always trimmed. In counterpoint the roses are full and the azaleas and trumpet vines add bright colors. A swath of hydrangeas stretches across the front lawn.

Whenever her job and the weather allow, Maiju is in the yard, gardening. "Sometimes I trim the hedge before it really needs it," she confessed, "so I can be in the fresh air. Gardening is kind of a natural thing. I never would want to live in an apartment without a garden. I need to be outside."

she has collected other old-fashioned varieties, including 'Sir Thomas Lipton,' 'Königin von Dänemark' (Queen of Denmark), and 'Madame Hardy.'

In the spring her beds are filled with yellow daffodils and the blue of grape hyacinth: "We always had that at home." She has thinned out the faded phlox and added other colors. "Now lots of gardeners have perennial beds, but when I first came to Minnesota, you never saw them," she said.

No garden chore intimidates Maiju. She's laid brick walkways through the yard and added a patio and seating area at the back door. She's installed wooden archways and planted climbing roses. On the east she's espaliered chestnut crabs. Though Maiju insists she has no special talent for this, the fact remains that espaliering is rare in gardens today because so much work and skill is involved.

Maiju's landscape, like her interior spaces, exemplifies the best of

Holding his niece, Chandia Kenyl, John Maire looks over the Sudanese farm near Elk River.
Photograph copyright 1998 Star Tribune/Minneapolis-St. Paul.

A SUDANESE DREAM

John Maire is a man on a mission. As director of SODA (Social Organization Development Agency), he envisions his fellow Sudanese immigrants as landowners and farmers. He sees them living in the country, where the children can run freely and the adults can raise and sell crops. The path is long, but Maire has taken the first steps in helping to organize a community-based farm in Elk River.

"Farming has been a part of African life from time immemorial," Maire said as he looked out over the one-acre plot of corn, green beans, cabbage, and hot peppers. "This has been our practice, our livelihood. It is what we know."

Nearly everyone in southern Sudan learns to farm, explained Maire, who now lives in Columbia Heights. "It is a communal way of living," he said. "Children observe and help their parents. Men prepare the ground and plant the seeds.

Women weed and harvest. Every day the women pick vegetables for the meal. It is a life we know and understand."

When immigrants come to the United States, they experience a "total cultural change," John said. "And the concept of having to work for money becomes the order of the day. They have to pay their bills, their debts. That is the Western way. They are almost completely cut off from their culture." With the Elk River farm, these immigrants, many refugees from war-torn Sudan, have the opportunity to reconnect with the land and with a culture they understand and love.

On acreage donated by local farmer Al Stewart, Maire and ten other Sudanese men prepared soil and planted seeds in the summer of 1998, singing in Swahili as they worked. The crops stretched out in long, straight rows to accommodate a donated tiller. "Back home we

don't plant in rows," John said. "We cast the seed in patches. When the weeds come, we just say, 'It's time to weed,' and people come to help."

In this, the first year, Maire and the others have harvested hundreds of pounds of produce—tomatoes and beans, kale and onions—and delivered the surplus to Sudanese in the Twin Cities. "Even though we got a late start, planting in June," John said, "we have raised so many vegetables. In one day we picked fifty pounds of jalapeños. East Africans love hot peppers."

John first left his country at age nine when his parents moved to Uganda because of the Sudan's

With the help of Alexander Hakim, one-year-old Chandia Kenyl is learning how to use a hoe. In Africa, very young children help out with the crops. Photograph copyright 1998 Star Tribune/Minneapolis-St. Paul.

upheaval. "The Sudan has been at war for the last sixty years," he explained, "but physically fighting for the last forty-three, so I was born and raised in that war. I had to stay in Uganda for seventeen years. From 1972 until 1982, there was relative peace in the Sudan. We saw a lot of development, and people were settling down. Schools started springing up and food was in abundance. I had my own business as an electrician."

After 1983, when fighting began once more between the Muslim north and the Christian and animist south, normal life became difficult. "I started working with the Sudan Council of Churches," explained John, "which was building the development arm of the church. We were engaged in constructing roads, building schools and hospitals, and establishing social education. My contribution of electrical work was seen as a rebellious act. When the war intensified, I thought there was no place for me. So I fled to Kenya and stayed there from 1991 until 1994. That year I came to North Dakota."

With his history, John could be embittered or discouraged, but he is neither. Instead, he is optimistic and excited about the possibilities of farming. "My father told me once that there is nothing impossible in this world as long as you set your mind to it," he said. "It doesn't matter how long it takes if you are determined to do it."

Such an attitude has served Maire well in setting up an office, informing the local Sudanese, learning about American farms, and meeting officials.

Though farming is an essential of Sudanese life, the Elk River farm was not part of SODA's original mission. The Anoka-based group was organized in 1997 to help Sudanese in their resettlement process, encouraging education, citizenship, and naturalization.

Before John Maire arrived in Minnesota, the federal Farm Extension Office had developed an outreach plan for Native Americans and for immigrants and refugees. In 1996, hundreds of black farmers demonstrated at the White House and brought a multimillion dollar lawsuit against the U.S. Department of Agriculture, claiming discrimination and unfair foreclosure of their farms. In response, the USDA

formed a Civil Rights Action Team and began working to encourage blacks and other people of color who had an interest in farming.

Thus was born in the spring of 1998 the Minnesota group, the Immigrant Farmers Coalition. Made up of Hmongs, Latinos, and Africans, the coalition was originally brought together by Don Hooker, of the state office of the Farm Service Agency, and John O'Donald, director of the Minnesota Food Association.

"There is a growing interest and concern about the large number of immigrants here," John said, "many of whom are doing low-income labor and who do not have access to proper training. We in the coalition started putting our heads together to see what would be the best approach to involving the immigrant communities in farming." John's work led him to folks involved in agriculture, locally and nationally.

In a short time, he and other Sudanese, including Duboul Deng and Alexander Hakim of SODA, made the farm a reality. "I can assure you," Maire said, "that up to this point all we have done is

Kale is one of the many crops on the Elk River site. This farm is planned as a commercial venture for the newly arrived Sudanese.

connect with people who were willing to help with certain equipment, tools, and even seeds. We were lucky. A farmer gave us seeds that were left over. He was going to throw them away.

"Don helped us get this land adjacent to the Farm Service Agency office. Being close to the agency has helped us a lot. They assisted with a tiller and put us in touch with a master gardener, who brought us a list of vegetables and their seasons. We also got some weeding and planting tools."

To inform their fellow Sudanese, Maire and the members of SODA used the African method: "We passed the word out," according to John. "That's the way we normally do in Africa, just tell people and they go and tell others." To build up interest for future years, they have invited other African groups—Somalis, Eritreans, and Kenyans—to come and partake of the harvest.

Dreaming big, Maire and his fellow organizers hope for more involvement in the years to come. They have joined local farmers' markets so growers can sell their crops. "Next year each gardening family will have its own plot," John explained. "They can grow whatever they wish and deal with the vegetables as they wish. We will just be there to oversee and help and make sure the plots are tended." They plan to organize a thanksgiving celebration when the crops are in.

Harvest Festival, *Golida,* is a high point of the year in the Sudan, John said. "Every day you will hear drum beats," he said. "Every day you will see dancing. We will be making a thanksgiving to God for the food. Then the village eats and celebrates for days and days. It is a time of recuperation after the exhaustion of harvest."

When you have left that rich life, John explained, "it is a vacuum, a complete vacuum. That is why we believe going back to the farm is the beginning of reclaiming all our cultural connectedness and *being* again. Those of us who have managed to go to the farm have already started feeling the completeness of ourselves."

Dr. Danuta Mazurek

INTENSIVELY POLISH

"Poland is one big flower bouquet," declared Dr. Danuta Mazurek. "The landscape is gorgeous, and the villages are charming and well-maintained. You see, these people are working people who take pride in where they live. They are embroidering. They are baking. They are decorating their homes. Maybe they have a two-by-four-foot garden in front of their little house, but it is full of flowers. We say 'without music, without flowers, and without our past, we don't exist, we don't exist.'"

When Dr. Mazurek came to Minnesota from the eastern part of Poland in the late 1960s, she was puzzled by American front lawns. "I wondered why people planted so many evergreens in their yards. Evergreens are for the forest. Where were the gardens?" She had left landscapes that were vastly different, functional as well as beautiful. Polish yards provided food along with beauty and opportunities for recreation. "What we have in Poland are decorative bushes, flowers, fruit trees, and fruit bushes," said Danuta. "Those are a must."

Dr. Mazurek's description of Polish yards fits her own property in Minneapolis, which, though small, is intensely gardened. Not one evergreen is to be seen. Danuta and her son, Ted, have provided spots for enjoying the garden: a lily pond, an eating area, a small square of grass. The remainder is devoted to flowers, fruits, and vegetables.

In 1985, when the family moved to their current house, they found a yard full of trees and debris, but little else. "It was pathetic," Dr. Mazurek said. She had the large cottonwoods removed because, she said, "I want a garden, not just shade." Her son built a fence for privacy.

Mazurek started initially with food crops. "I just decided to put in currants, because that's fruit, then gooseberries, raspberries, and my first cherry tree. In the back I had my vegetable garden. That was the beginning.

"In the front I started from a three-by-three plot on the south corner, then came digging slowly up to the end," she said with a laugh. Danuta may have been digging slowly, but she was digging continuously. In short order, she converted a neglected lot into a beauty spot. "Some neighbors have said I made a heaven of hell," she said.

Mazurek started with alpines in the front because they are at their

147

fresh and for canning. "If Polish people do not have borscht at Christmas, we will die," she said. She grows cucumbers for pickling. "Just use water, salt, dill, garlic, and leaves of the cherry for your pickles," she advised. "Don't use vinegar—that destroys vitamins."

Danuta gets large harvests of tomatoes from a few plants (probably that healthy soil again). From July until frost she has cherry tomatoes, plus slices of 'Big Boy' and beefsteak for salads and sandwiches. "I prefer the beefsteak because it's sweeter," she said. "This summer I harvested a two-pounder." In the fall she extracts and cans the juice, and "puts up" stewed tomatoes. "It's so good to pull out this juice in the middle of winter," she said.

Her fruit collection would be an accomplishment on any lot; on this modest property it is especially impressive. There are strawberries and raspberries, which yield bowl after bowl of sweet fruit throughout the summer. She grows rhubarb for

Because she improves her soil continually with manure and compost, Dr. Mazurek gets healthy crops of vegetables and fruit. Here, a tomato weighs in at two pounds.

jam and sauce, as well as three kinds of currants: white, black, and red. "The jam from currants is fantastic," Mazurek said.

She has two gooseberry bushes. "Gooseberries are terrific for wine," she emphasized, "especially when you put black currants with them. Or you can eat the berries fresh; they are sweet and delicious."

There are several fruit trees—a pear, three cherries, and a plum. "I had an apple, but it had too many bug problems, so I took it out. I don't want to use chemicals on my food. Chemicals here are an obsession," she added. "In Poland we have alternative methods."

Her cellar is lined with row upon row of glass jars, sparkling with the bright colors of summer: the green of pickles and beans, the red of cherry preserves and tomatoes, the orange of pumpkin, and the ruby tones of beets and strawberry-rhubarb jam.

How did Dr. Mazurek become accomplished at caring for the garden and preserving its bounty? "You know," she told a visitor, "I was just looking at what people were doing. In Poland, our kids are always with their parents. They are

ALPINES

Alpine is the generic term applied to all plants that grow above the tree line in mountainous areas. However, it has come to mean a large range of small, hardy plants and bulbs, mostly perennial. They can be grown in natural habitats like woodland gardens, or in man-made rock gardens, alpine houses, or raised beds.

These perennials have adapted to their mountainous terrain in several ways. They have tap roots that penetrate more than a foot of soil. Most are very short, often ground-hugging (this helps them avoid the full force of the wind). Generally, they have small, compact leaves, which require little energy to maintain. They flower early, because the mountain summer season is short.

observing and they are getting assignments—'Here, you try this row and see what happens.' That's the normal pattern of raising kids. We don't have any little princesses of Daddy, but children who are helping out."

Obviously, Dr. Mazurek's childhood lessons "took." Her colorful, well-tended property stands out on a street of aging homes. Not content with the status quo, she has plans for the future. She's redoing the strawberry beds to accommodate some "everbearers." "This new kind will give fruit four times," she said. And she's pulling out all the

alpines to renew the soil and get rid of weeds. "You have to do this in fall," she insisted, "or you'll interrupt the bulbs blooming."

The careful attention Mazurek gives her plants explains their health and abundance. She has another explanation: "I put a lot of love into the garden and somehow my flowers listen to me."

Ludmila and Leonid Bryskin

THE SHORTEST GROWING SEASON

Ludmila Bryskin knows how to propagate her currant bushes by layering—bending a branch to earth and covering it with soil until it forms roots. She has increased her stock many times this way. Similarly, she can multiply her strawberry plants to trade with friends. She has learned that seeds will germinate very quickly if they are kept moist, wrapped in plastic, and carried close to her heart. "The temperature is uniformly warm," she explained, "and you soon forget they are there. Old ladies know that tip." She knows that black currant leaves give pickles a nice flavor and that horseradish leaves keep them crisp.

Her husband, Leonid, learned several ways to stretch the short Russian growing season. While it was still snowing, he dug a fairly deep trench in the ground and put manure inside. On top he placed leaves or hay and covered the whole thing with soil. As the manure decomposed, it generated heat, making an area where the Bryskins could plant early seeds and get excellent germination. "It was important to start early," she said, "to make the most out of our little bit of earth."

At their dacha, ("our cabin") outside of St. Petersburg, Ludmila said, "we had no gas, no running water, no plumbing. Telephones were unheard of. Water was well water, collected in buckets." To make life a little more convenient, Leonid rigged up an aboveground watering system, which brought water from the well to the cabin. "He just made it himself with pipes and a pump he built. The water came into a big barrel. We felt that was so sophisticated," Ludmila said.

Ludmila is modestly surprised that Americans consider this knowledge and these skills so "special and unusual. They ask, 'How is it you know all that?' But really, this is so natural, so general. Does someone have to teach you how to paint? No, you just pick up a brush and start painting.

"There so many people were gardening. You see others. You try. You ask. You compare. We were always exchanging information and materials. Someone comes by to see what you have. Then they tell you they have an excellent strawberry, very juicy, very productive. Would you like to trade?"

In addition to receiving over-the-fence information, Ludmila read and studied ways to improve her crops, because gardening in Russia was a

Horseradish is a multipurpose plant. The leaves go in Ludmila's pickles; the roots are grated and combined with apples, vinegar, and bit of sugar for a tasty side dish.

serious undertaking. "We could survive without a garden, in the sense that we wouldn't have died from starvation," she said. "But not much was available. It really helped us to get fresh produce, so we grew everything—all kinds of vegetables, of course, but also cooking herbs, different varieties of apples, plums, currants, and berries."

The Bryskins started early (with Leonid's heat trench), worked the land intensively, and made the season last. "The land our garden was on was very small," Ludmila said. "It was given to my husband's family by the state. But we didn't own it and we couldn't add to it. So we did try to utilize every bit of it." When one crop finished, like the early spring radishes and green onions, another took its place. Two small greenhouses helped tomatoes and cucumbers ripen in the cool fall weather.

The garden and life at the dacha were especially important to the Bryskins because they needed to get their two children out of the polluted city. "The air was so bad that it was affecting everybody," Ludmila said, "but mostly the kids. So children had a lot of diseases.

It was always recommended to give them vitamins, and everybody tried to take their kids out of the city for the summer.

"In Russia everybody lived together. It was not like here, but a much closer family. In the summer our children and their grandparents would stay at the dacha, and my husband and I came out on weekends. We had to grow all the vegetables there because in the rural areas there are no stores.

"Here in America, you go anywhere and there is a Super America," she said with a laugh. "There, in the city stores are poorly stocked. In the country it's like a different century."

Ludmila became a gardener after the birth of her first child. "I was a town girl, totally," she said. "My mother-in-law used to do the gardening. When we had a child, she began to care for him so I could keep my job. I was grateful for her help. Then it became my task to take care of the garden."

Weekends were filled with cooking for the week ahead, washing clothes (without benefit of a machine), and gardening. "At first, I hated it, but there was a purpose,"

Just as he did every fall in Russia, Leonid makes a trench in which to bury his compost and leaves. As they decompose, they give off heat, allowing the Bryskins to plant seeds early. The couple has made their soil rich and productive in just a few seasons.

SORREL
(Rumex)

Sorrel has grown wild for hundreds of years in the meadows and woodlands of Europe, Asia, and North America. In the spring, when at its youngest and mildest, sorrel is used in salads and soups, and is cooked as a green. As it matures, the leaves become more acidic and can be used to flavor cream soups or as an accompaniment to meats. Sorrel leaves are shaped like spinach and range from pale to dark green in color.

Rich in potassium and vitamins A and C, sorrel has a sour, lemony taste. The leaves are said to quench thirst and reduce fevers, and they are taken as a diuretic tea. Herbalists use a leaf poultice to treat acne, mouth ulcers, boils, and infected wounds.

French sorrel. Photograph by David Cavagnaro.

she said. "I knew it was necessary, so I did it. You know, maybe I would have liked to read a book or relax. Instead, I was thinning, or aerating, or harvesting. Our gardening was very labor-intensive," she added, almost superfluously.

"Now," she said, "they have a fancy word for what we did—*sustainable agriculture*. We never used any chemicals. Our neighbor had animals, so we got that manure. Nearby there were gypsies, and they had horses. Years ago Khrushchev prohibited horses. Only gypsies were allowed to keep them because it was considered their mode of life. We would pay them something for their manure. And, of course, we composted."

As the years of gardening continued, Ludmila came to enjoy the work and to know many ways to bring in excellent yields. She and Leonid gathered moss from the forest floor to spread between the strawberries. "That way the fruit stays clean," she explained, "and the leaves remain drier and less likely to get diseased."

The Bryskins collected wood ashes to dust the crops. "They have many minerals and micronutrients.

Ash from wood is also the best pesticide. We always covered the strawberries with the ash so they wouldn't get insects."

Because large, healthy crops were essential, the Bryskins were very attentive to the plants, observing their needs and their performance. "When you multiplied your strawberries, you only used runners from the best plants," she said. "And when you saved seeds, you took them from your tastiest, most productive crops. I really think we improved our seed stock over the years."

In the early 1990s, all the Bryskins—grandparents, parents, and the two children—emigrated to Minnesota. "We are Jewish people, Jewish only because of a stamp on the passport," said Ludmila. "When we grew up, everything was prohibited, even dangerous. There was no religion, no observances. But you know, when the economy goes down, you have to blame somebody, so the anti-Semitism became much worse. We wanted to give our children better opportunities, and we came here."

The Bryskins have made a good life in New Hope, but six and a half years later, Ludmila is still surprised by the contrasts between Russia and America. "Here you can find anything. Strawberries grown in California are in Minnesota the next day. In Russia they were never available. And the roads—even in the forest here they are better than those going to our dacha."

Though such conveniences make life easier, they have their downside, Ludmila noted gently. "I think that here people take so many things for granted, and unfortunately it makes them less creative. In Russia you had to be creative to survive." So, despite such shortcuts at hand, the Bryskins delight in making do, re-using and improving what they have.

They continue to garden with enthusiasm and resourcefulness. "Because we have so much shade, we don't grow as much, but every year we add more," said Ludmila. Besides culinary herbs, salad greens, cucumbers, tomatoes ("I raise those from seed"), and beets, they have three kinds of berries. "We have raspberries and a strawberry bed. We're trying blueberries because in Russia you could only get wild ones. I've been looking for red currants, which were very popular

in Russia, very productive and easy to grow." They are growing the perennial sorrel *(Rumex)*, which was in many Russian gardens, but is hard to find in Minnesota. "It's full of vitamins," said Ludmila. "I don't know why people here don't grow it."

The Bryskins' main difficulties have been shade and poor, claylike soil. Every summer they hack out roots and add humus. "We gather all our leaves and those from the neighbors," she said. "It's a lot, almost two yards high. In spring, when they've compressed and decomposed, we turn them in.

"We do compost all our kitchen waste, which we did in Russia. Even in winter we put the peelings and eggshells in two big containers, which we cover and keep outside. With the cold, there is no smell, no bugs."

Just as he did at the dacha, Leonid makes a trench in spring and adds the food waste, covering it with dry leaves or hay and then soil. "Really," said Ludmila, "it decomposes quickly. If you put your hand in, you can feel the heat." After only a few years, their soil has become dark and productive. "We

don't use commercial fertilizer. I'm very conscious about pesticides on the things you eat," Ludmila explained.

The Bryskins are knowledgeable about herbal medicine, using chamomile, burdock, and mints. They collect linden flowers for tea. One plant they know in Russia as *mate matcheba* is good for gout and arthritis. "We are trying to grow it here, but it struggles," she said.

In explaining her devotion to gardening, Ludmila is a bit amazed. "I'm surprised myself," she said. "When we came here, I realized it was not necessry. Yet each year we take more ground into the garden. In Russia we had to raise food, and it took years before I enjoyed it. Now I'm doing it for pleasure. You know, material things cannot fulfill you. Doing this I am rewarded."

Peace in
the Garden

Ben Carrasca

WHEN THE EAST MEETS DULUTH

n a Duluth neighborhood of conventional lawns, Ben Carrasca's yard stands out. One first notices the elegant pagoda-like gate at the streetside parking bay. Nearby, the welcome lamp has been fitted with a wooden frame. Ferns and bamboo tubes of various sizes encircle its base. Paths marked off with stones lead the visitor through several minilandscapes: waterfall, pond, look-out point, sand garden. The Asian style introduced at the gate is evident throughout the yard.

The whole is Ben's handiwork, a project that started modestly enough seven years ago and now encompasses all his property. "When we bought the house," he explained, "our children were grown-up. I would come home at noon from my job as a baker and have several hours alone before my wife returned. That's when I started to enjoy gardening."

Over the years, Ben has gradually replaced most of his lawn with intricately designed gardens and seating areas. Each cluster contains plants and objects arranged to complement one another—a mounded lady's mantle against the stiff-leafed iris, shiny hosta beneath a dark arborvitae, low wooden fences as accents. Everywhere are small details to capture the eye.

The garden is a complex of shapes and textures, but its design has taken shape through years of hands-on work, rather than through a formal plan. "There's nothing written down," explained Ben, "but I see things in my head."

Much of the landscape he has created reminds him of his childhood home in Batac in the Philippines. "Visitors may see a lot that's beautiful," he said, "a rock, the arrangement of a plant. What they can't see is that often these things

Young Ben on a veranda in the Philippines. Photograph courtesy of Ben Carrasca.

Ben has created a number of small landscapes on his lot. Here a wooden bridge crosses a dry streambed. The inspirations come from the Asian gardens he has observed.

are from my past. Perhaps they're done as my mother did them." The plants are not necessarily the same, because tropical plants won't grow in Minnesota, but they call to mind the ones that grew on the islands. "I may not have a pineapple—there are pineapples everywhere in Batac," he said, "but I can grow things that look pineapply.

Thirty years ago, Ben left Batac for Duluth because his brother was stationed at the U.S. Air Force base north of town. "Our dad was in the U.S. Army," he explained, "so we were all American citizens. We had to come here for a time or lose our citizenship."

Carrasca arrived at age nineteen, married a Duluth woman a few years later, and remained to raise their family. Later he graduated from the University of Minnesota at Duluth in sociology and criminology. When jobs in his field were tight, he found work as a baker, and for a time owned a bakery. "It's been a good life for me," he said. "Duluth is a beautiful place to live."

Beautiful Duluth may be, but Ben has carried around other notions of beauty from his boyhood in the tropics. Recent trips to Batac with

The details in Carrasca's garden are all-important, inviting visitors to pause and take notice.

his second wife, Carol, have kept those ideas fresh. His own garden has brought a bit of the Philippines to northern ground. And though he can identify some Asian influences in his landscape, Ben was not consciously trying to recreate Batac, but simply gardening as he wanted to. "I didn't learn these things in a book," he said by way of explanation. "They just came to me."

For a small yard, there is much to see: a fountain in the midst of a rock-lined pond, the delicate teahouse with a patterned stone floor, groupings of dramatic grasses and colorful shrubs. Ben finds the arrangement reminiscent of Batac, where "the lots are smaller and everything is crammed in. People love to garden in the Philippines," he said, "but there is definitely not a formal style like the English perennial border."

For many Westerners, Ben explained, gardening is just about

163

plants. "That's only part of the picture," he said. "The way plants are spaced, how they relate to objects like lanterns or pots, and how rocks are used are equally important."

To Carrasca, plants are almost accessories. He may not even know their names, but he selects them from nursery stock if he likes their color, shape, or texture. When they don't work in one spot, he moves them to another. If plants are garden elements here, flowers are only occasional accents, often added to please his wife. Ben prefers the subtle shades of green, gray, and beige, and he chooses plants more for their form and size than for their bloom.

Rarely does he leave a plant by itself, instead placing something (a bamboo tube, a wooden lantern) next to it for contrast. "I tell people that a plant is like a beautiful woman," he explained. "She is lovely by herself, but adding a scarf enhances her beauty. So placing a

Ben enjoys the interplay of stone and gravel textures and colors with the various hues and forms of conifers and herbaceous plants.

carefully chosen rock next to a plant can bring out its color or make it look larger."

Rocks are also selected for color and form. "When people come to look at the garden, they may just see a pile of rocks," Ben said. "What they don't know is that I might take half a day to find the exact placement that works." Ever on the lookout, he's amassed an interesting collection, from jagged gray stones to smooth boulders. One rounded beige piece looks uncannily like a small hippo.

The satisfactions of his garden are many, Ben will attest. Working with his hands, whether hauling rocks or trimming a plant, is always a pleasure. Lately he has come to enjoy all the visitors his place attracts. "Several years ago my garden won third place in the Duluth garden contest," he said. "Ever since, we have had tour buses and other visitors. They appreciate what they see and say nice things. Sometimes I hear older gardeners wondering about my arrangements, why I don't line things up. And sometimes I think they get the big picture, but don't see the details. When they come back for the second and

third time, then they begin to see the small things."

Carrasca's greatest satisfaction is also the hardest to explain, he said, taking care to get the phrases right. "Working outside gives you a lot of time to think," he said. "Along the way it teaches you patience." The Western mind would say that gardening is "relaxing," Ben said, "but that's not quite right. It's hard for an Asian to convey this to a Westerner, but gardening brings harmony, peace. We call it balance. There are a lot of uncertainties, a lot of problems in the world. When you spend half a day in your garden, you get some perspective. Somewhere in your thinking, you come to a solution, or else you see that there is none. You begin to see the small things."

Rosa Garcia-Peltoniemi

HAVANA HEALING

s a young girl in Havana, Rosa Garcia-Peltoniemi gardened in a backyard filled with fruit trees. Even now, nearly thirty years later, she can remember the exact placement of the huge mango, the bananas, the small Spanish cherry, the *sapota (Pouteria)*, and the hibiscus hedge. She can recall the way the mango tree branches spilled over the wall from her neighbor's yard and how the sweetsop tree gave such good fruit. "I loved my garden because it was so secluded and peaceful," she explained. "The space was very small, but intensely cultivated."

It was there, as she planted flowers and endlessly arranged marble paving stones around the cherry tree, that Rosa found respite from the political oppression visited on her family. "When the Cuban revolution began," she said, "my parents were very active supporters. But as the regime turned commu-

nist, they became disenchanted, so our lives changed completely. Even though they didn't work against the government, they were branded opponents and dissidents."

Those were years of "high alert, crisis," she said, with the Garcias always under surveillance. There was no way to protect children from feeling the dangers: "The adults were talking about the situation all the time, and we would hear."

Governmental disapproval was intensified because her father's family was in the book business. "All sorts of books were prohibited, common ones as well as classics," Rosa recalled, "and there was always the fear that officials would sweep through the house in search of offending titles." To foil the searchers, Rosa's mother would gather up the books and the olive oil (illegal because it was bought on the black market) and carefully lower her brother, oil in hand, over

Rosa in her walled Cuban garden. Photograph courtesy of Rosa Garcia-Peltoniemi.

the back wall. Then she would throw the books over after him.

By 1965, when Rosa was twelve, the family decided that there was no possible future for them in Cuba and they requested permission to emigrate to America. "The Cuban government made us wait five years," she said, "and we were always under suspicion. The experience really shaped our lives."

As the child of dissidents, Rosa wasn't allowed to participate in many activities. "Because of the great distrust of our neighbors, my family was isolated and cut off from normal life," she explained. That's when she began working daily within the high walls of her backyard. "I took a lot of comfort from gardening," she said. "The front yard was public; we could be seen. But in the backyard I could feel some privacy and safety. I spent hours and hours moving the pavers and planting flowers. It helped me pass the time of waiting."

Having healing plants in the garden is important to Rosa. Here, foxgloves (Digitalis) *make an early summer appearance with astilbes.*

SWEET CICELY
(*Myrrhis odorata*)

native of Great Britain, this aromatic herb derives its Latin name from the Greek word for perfume because of its myrrh-like smell. It was used in former times as a salad herb with a mild anise flavor. The peeled roots can be boiled and eaten as a vegetable; the seeds add flavor to fruit salads. All parts are edible. In fact, old herbalists describe the plant as "so harmless you cannot use it amiss." Given to "old people that are dull and without courage," it was said that it "comforteth the heart and increaseth their lust and strength." The plant was useful in other ways, as well—helpful in pleurisy, effective for consumption, and able to ease gout and ulcers.

Whatever its medicinal value, the herb, with its bright green, fern-like leaves and masses of creamy white flowers, is stunning in bloom and handsome throughout the season. One of the first nectar plants to appear in the spring, sweet Cicely is attractive to bees, butterflies, and hummingbirds.

Sweet Cicely (Myrrhis odorata). *Photograph by David Cavagnaro.*

Today in Minnesota, her plants and the climate are vastly different, but once again Rosa's garden provides a sense of peace and harmony. In her work as a psychotherapist and the director of client services at the Minnesota Center for Victims of Torture, Garcia-Peltoniemi counsels survivors of political torture—a rewarding job, but one in which progress is slow and the stresses are many.

"My garden is a bit of a metaphor for what I do at the center," she said, "but one in which the results come, not only more quickly, but more palpably. I find it very satisfying to plant a seed and watch it mature into a beautiful flower."

The long backyard border glows with bloom throughout the season. Spring tulips, daffodils, and lilies of the valley give way to rhododendrons and violets. Antique roses, among them 'Therese Bugnet,' 'Sarah Van Fleet,' and 'Rosa Alba,' make a June showing. White Asiatic lilies, cleome, balloon flower, and hollyhocks add color in July and August. Rocks, salvaged from construction sites, line the curving bed.

For Garcia-Peltoniemi, the emotional content of a garden is as important as its beauty. So amid the ferns and hollyhocks, she grows the "ancient healing herbs," as she calls them, plants with names like germander and *Myrhhis odorata*. There are rue and angelica, herbs that suggest good fortune, and two kinds of mint, both known in Spanish as *yerba buena*, "the good herb." Pink malva, with its "benevolent virtues," and pastel foxgloves *(Digitalis)* provide July blossoms. The broad gray pads of mullein and lamb's ears, once used to bind up wounds, now blend and soften the mass of green.

Indeed, on closer examination, it becomes apparent that this is a garden of blooming herbs, with other perennials grown as fillers. "I am in the healing business," Rosa explained. "But also I come from a culture in which herbs and plants are very much a part of daily life—chamomile to settle the stomach, the flowers of the linden tree to calm the nerves. Even though I don't use the herbs myself, this whole notion of ancient plants used for healing and well-being is most interesting to me."

And as Rosa lovingly pronounces "hyssop" and "sweet Cicely," "lady's mantle" and "echinacea," the listener can easily believe in their beneficial qualities.

Lilies have always looked tropical to Rosa; they remind her of her Cuban childhood.

The herb border may be Rosa's largest plot, but she tends other gardens and gardens in the making. There is the healthy sunflower plot she shares with Alejandro, her four-year-old son ("I am trying to encourage his interest in the garden"), and her varied indoor plant collection. "Coming from the warm tropics, I find it difficult to withstand a long winter with no vegetation," she said. "So I must have a house filled with greenery and bloom."

Here, among her potted plants, Garcia-Peltoniemi indulges her fondness for tropical greenery, nursing along a cut-leaved papaya tree and a clump of Cuban oregano *(Plectranthus amboinicus)*, with its handsome foliage. A large fuchsia and a graceful coffee tree brighten indoor spaces with their dark, glossy leaves. Red peppers and lemon verbena add spice to the kitchen garden. A flourishing sapota, now two feet tall, stands as a reminder of Havana days. "I may not get fruit, but I do expect blossom," said Rosa. Like many gardeners, she treasures plants from friends. A client from Southeast Asia contributed seeds for the pummelo tree

(Citrus grandis); a neighbor moving to D.C. left a peace lily. It's a collection to admire, but Rosa would like more. "If we ever win the lottery," she will tell you, "we would add a solarium."

Just now, a garden in the making looms large with Rosa. As always, her husband, Eric, has helped with the construction, moving large mounds of dirt and transplanting shrubs. But Rosa has responsibility for the design. The new garden will be built around three major plants: antique and shrub roses for Rosa's father, the peonies of Eric's grandmother, and white Asiatic lilies, which she herself loves.

The deep reds and velvety whites will certainly make an elegant garden. But as in the herb border, Rosa chose the plants as much for their meaning as for their beauty. "My father died recently," she explained. "He was originally from Spain, where roses are a favorite flower. They were his favorites as well. In looking at them, I am reminded of him and of my European heritage. With the peonies we remember Eric's Finnish family, and lilies I have always loved because they look tropical to me."

"Obviously, living here I cannot garden as I would in Cuba," Garcia-Peltoniemi said. "The aesthetics are totally different. There's a certain lushness to the tropics that is very appealing to me. None of that can be transplanted or brought back. Still, the desire to have vegetation indoors, the love of blooming plants, the knowledge of herbs—these are all things I have brought with me."

Clearly the garden is a lovely and loving connection with the best of Rosa's past. In searching for stones and planting heirloom roses, she has created a place of beauty and memory to share with Eric and Alejandro, just as her family shared their enthusiasms with her. Perhaps little "Ale" may one day decide to pass on the tradition. Meanwhile, something of the young Rosa continues to be expressed in her ardent nurturing of floral space.

Lucille and Clyde Estey

THE CIRCLE OF LIFE

hat's the thing about plants, every one has a purpose to it," said Clyde Estey, pointing to the brilliant yarrow. "You can use these leaves for tea and also rub them on for a bug repellent. The monarda, Oswego tea, here is a good medicine plant. All the mints are really good for stomach problems." As he walked from bed to bed in his large yard, Estey thoughtfully touched each plant, discussing its uses and horticultural needs with the detail of a scientist.

At seventy-seven, Clyde has a lot of experience with plants, and it shows. "I learned about gardening from my family," said Clyde, who grew up and still lives on the White Earth Reservation. "It was something that we depended on. Times were tough. At one time, everybody in the village had a garden. My mother put up about a thousand quarts of produce, so you know those gardens meant a lot. And, of

course, every one of us kids had our rows to tend. We did our part.

"Then, later, I did gardening for the government nurse who lived out here. But ever since Lucille and I married, we've had a garden. I like to experiment and try different things."

Clyde went on to describe the traditional circle plots of Native American agriculture. "Twenty-five years ago I was planting in circles," he said. "The peas and beans were growing up the corn. Potatoes were on the ground. All the vegetables were in circles. We raised a lot of stuff that way. And you could put all the weeds in the middle. I knew that planting close together like that, you needed to feed it, so I gave it some manure. But I never even knew at that time that it was traditional. Then last summer, here comes a lady, from Michigan, I believe, teaching that circle gardening is the traditional Native

American way. And I thought, I didn't need somebody to teach me," Clyde said good-naturedly. "I'd already figured it out."

Clyde still does some gardening in circles, especially the corn and squash. But since he's an experimenter, there's much more. Clyde and Lucille have numerous large flower beds on their property, each with its own style. Lucille is working on a shade bed under the trees and a plot of hybridized daylilies in a sunny spot. Near the house a long perennial border is filled with Asiatic lilies, liatris, echinops, and old-fashioned roses. ("I just kept

Clyde practiced circle gardening long before the experts promoted it. In this bed, the squash is growing between cornstalks, to the benefit of each.

dividing one old rose to get all these," Clyde said.) A raised island bed out front holds dogwood, red barberry, spirea, and Andorra juniper. Hollyhocks, clematis, and brown-eyed Susans add color against the house.

Dotted throughout the yard are bird feeders and houses that Clyde has constructed from tree stumps, metal parts, and weathered wood. Drawn by the abundant water and food, butterflies and birds are constantly swooping through the yard.

The Esteys rarely purchase vegetables because they raise so many

crops, everything from beans to kohlrabi to watermelons. Their good soil is made even richer with well-rotted manure from a neighboring farm, their own compost, and leaf mold from the forest ("it's just like 100 percent fertilizer").

"People don't realize how much stuff you can grow in just a little bitty area," Clyde said. "It can help you out financially, but also healthwise. You're getting fresh produce and you know there's no chemicals in it. That's the beauty of it. The government outlawed DDT in the U.S., but manufacturers are still

selling it overseas. It comes back to us on the vegetables we get in the grocery store."

Clyde feels passionately about helping others get started with gardening and has taught hundreds of young people. "I think we have to work with the kids," he said. "They come in by the busload here to look at what we grow. We try to encourage them. Their parents don't garden, so they don't know the first thing about it, but they're interested."

Recently the Esteys, who are both master gardeners, began working with the Aki Project (*Aki* means "land" in Ojibwe) to promote community gardening at White Earth. They've donated part of their land for a huge plot, and both are on the Aki advisory board. The project is funded by the University of Minnesota, the University Extension Service, and the Bush Foundation. "There's a lot of diabetes on the reservation," Clyde said. "This is a way to help Native Americans

The Esteys' house is surrounded by flowers. On a late summer day, the intense pink of malva adds to the glow.

LABRADOR TEA
(Ledum latifolium)

abrador tea *(Ledum latifolium)*, also known as Saint James Tea, is a fragrant, evergreen shrub of the heath family. The plant has irregular, woolly branches, oblong leaves, and large, white flowers. The three-to-five-foot plant grows in cold bogs and mountain woods and is native to Greenland, Labrador, and Nova Scotia, as well as to the northern United States. Labrador tea is an important component of woodland understories and is often abundant in the shaded portions of the forest. In some states, it is considered rare or threatened.

During the American War of Independence, the leaves were much used instead of tea leaves. They have a pleasant odor, a spicy taste, and have been used medicinally for coughs and sore throats. Strewn among clothes, they will keep away moths. In Lapland, branches are placed among grain to repel mice. A strong solution will kill lice.

Labrador tea. Photograph by David Cavagnaro.

improve their diet, to start eating vegetables again. The planting and weeding is supposed to be a community effort, and then everyone can come and share the harvest. It seems like the interest is growing.

There are eight community plots and about four hundred small home gardens that we know about."

Estey can speak eloquently about gardening: "Here you take a little seed and put it in the ground and it multiplies. You're getting so much out of that, you know. That's a miracle." But his rich relationship with plants goes beyond the garden. The Esteys can and freeze produce— "It's so easy to do," he insisted. He gathers medicinal plants in the nearby woods and wetlands. "In June that small cattail has a seed that's got a lot of vitamins in it," he explained. "And I picked a lot of those, some fifty bags. Then I made a cattail muffin that everybody likes. Of course, I wait till after they've eaten them, and then I say, 'Do you know what you just ate?' The cattail seed's got a flavor all its own—kind of nutty."

Clyde also dries plants. "Here is the red clover," he said, pointing out a table of the drying blossoms. "This is one of the best plants there is for cancer. We make a tea out of it." Hanging in bunches were many others he had grown or collected: wild garlic ("very powerful"), pennyroyal, vervain, catnip, hyssop, wild ginger, Oswego tea, and spearmint ("from a really old plant that's been here fifty years"). On other days, still more plants go into Clyde's teas: wild raspberry, chokecherry, and Labrador tea *(Ledum latifolium)*. "We get it from the swamp," he said.

"There's so many of these plants, like the white pine and the slippery elm, that are good for several things," he said. "You take the cambium layer and use it and it makes terrific tea. It's also good for poultices.

"I like to look at the medicinal uses of plants both ways—what the Europeans used them for and what the Indians said about them. It's good to compare. I have two or three books and they all say pretty much the same thing."

Plants even figure prominently in Clyde's craft work, basketry. To him, the craft is much more than weaving the reeds together. First, Clyde must find the right tree. "You need growth rings about the thickness of a quarter so you can resplit them," he explained. Then he drags the log back to his workshop where the growth rings are split off and pounded on a form. Some will be dyed to give color to the designs.

"I learned this from Lucille's mother when she was eighty," Clyde said. "I could see that the skill would die with her, because no one else was taking it up."

"She was a real artist," Lucille added, pulling out some pictures of her mother's intricate work. "Some of her baskets are in the Smithsonian."

For a time Clyde was the only person on three reservations making baskets, but now his son, Brad, and grandson, Ryan, have also taken it up. "There's a lot of work to it, I guess," Clyde explained. "Not many people are willing to go into the mosquito-filled woods, look for a tree, and drag it out. Not many women have the strength to do that."

Estey's life shows the genuineness of his devotion to the plants that surround him, wild and cultivated. He knows their benefits to him and his family, and he works hard to spread the word to others. When you're attentive to the natural world around you, he explained, you're always engaged, interested. "My big thing is just to go out there in the morning and just walk around and see new life. Here we've got a new flower coming up. We've got new plants coming in the garden. You know, that's something to see."

Toulia Dennis

HOT! HOT! HOT!

n West Africa, Toulia Dennis's life was intimately tied to crops and food production. The Dennises raised pineapples, citrus fruits, bananas, sugarcane, and rubber plants on their farm. At home they grew vegetables, more pineapples, and the beloved soursop tree *(Annona muricata),* with its tart fruit. There were shrubs on the lawn and "oh, so many flowers, flowers, flowers," said Toulia in her melodic Liberian accent. "I was on an acre of land in Monrovia, and on an acre of land, you can grow a lot."

"In West Africa where I come from," said Toulia by way of explanation, "most homes really do have their gardens. When we were growing up, my mother taught us to grow all our own vegetables right around the house."

Because labor was inexpensive there, the Dennises employed workers to help with yard and field work, but every Friday the whole family headed outside the city to work on the farm. Along with the others, Toulia planted, fertilized, and harvested. "We all worked hard, hard," she remembered. A typical harvest yielded thirty one-hundred-pound sacks of oranges and grapefruits.

Toulia can trace her affinity for the land back to her grandfather, who came to Africa from South Carolina. "He never lived in a city," she said, "but went up-country and into the hinterlands. He just made farms. So we all grew up with our arms outstretched to agriculture."

No doubt this early connection to food production made Toulia's choice of career a natural one. As an adult she became a nutritionist, working for over twenty-five years in the Executive Mansion (the home and office of Liberia's president, the locus of political power) and the West African Insurance College. Even today her conversation is laced with references to the vitamin content of food and what constitutes a healthy diet. "Green bananas are very nutritious," she will tell you, "they have 30 to 40 percent iron. We boil the plantains and feed them to babies when they are small." And "the leaves of the cassava are medicinal." And again, "the soursop fruit gives you about 60 percent of the vitamin C you need."

Though she believes in the nutritional value of homegrown produce, Dennis has always felt the spiritual importance of gardens. In Liberia her plots were a respite from long

pineapple," she said, "to see what I can achieve."

But her "main line," as she says, is the habañero pepper (one of the hottest peppers known) "because it's so difficult to get here," she said. "All Africans like peppers, especially the hot peppers. They use them as the base for sauces and to season the foods. We haven't had the habañero at home [in Africa]; we had the typical African pepper. But I'm trying this for an experiment."

Dennis starts her seeds in the basement in late spring and plants about twenty plants. "I tell you, I get a whole lot of peppers from that," she said. "When harvest time comes, I have a lot of produce to give to my friends."

Besides providing bounty to share with others and foods for special dishes, her garden is a place of comfort. "While my mother-in-law was alive," Toulia said, "I would take her out into the yard and the flowers and vegetables were growing and blooming all around her. She

The roses Toulia grows in Minnesota are a palpable reminder of her Liberian gardens.

was so delighted—she was just new. She reminisced about her life in Africa."

The special pressures of an immigrant household keep Toulia from doing all the gardening she would like. She cares for her elderly mother, several family members, and a constant stream of friends and relatives, and her own health is not the best. Yet she handles it all as she must have managed the large farm in Liberia, with grace, good humor, and an air of calm.

"Women are very, very strong in Liberia," Toulia said, her explanation making it clear she means physically as well as mentally. "At home you don't buy a house, you build it yourself out of concrete blocks. Most women oversee the construction of their own structures. I had a six-bedroom house and I made every block with my own hands."

Today her challenges may be as much mental as physical, but Toulia meets them with the same determination. "You don't just give up, you don't give up," she insisted, "because most of the time when you give up, you're giving another person the opportunity to also give

up. And that someone needs to be inspired, needs to be encouraged. They need to know that they can also pick up and make the best of their life.

"That's why I look so forward to gardening. To me it is renewal, a reawakening of your whole outlook in life. It brings back to you the joy, the inspiration. I tell people, it's like a peaceful solution. You work and then in the end you see exactly what you work for. You get up in the morning and you see the roses are blooming. And you say to yourself, 'Isn't it wonderful what Nature can do for us?'"

Pradip and Gita Kar

JASMINE AND GERANIUMS

asmine, bougainvillea, "queen of the night," honeycreeper—their names evoke a vine-laden paradise, heavy with sweet fragrance. This is the landscape of India, birthplace of Gita and Pradip Kar, where a plant's perfume may be even lovelier than its form. Here, flowering trees called 'Flame of the Forest' (*Butea monosperma*), 'Golden Shower' (*Cassia fistula*), 'Pride of India' (*Lagerstroemia speciosa*), and 'Rusty Shield Bearer' (*Peltophorum pterocarpa*) light up the countryside with blossoms of dazzling red and bright yellow.

Here too grow so many varieties of jasmine that the plant cannot be called simply jasmine, as is the practice in America, but *balephool* or *mogra* or *juhi*. "The moment we say the word *mogra*, each of us is thinking the same thing," explained Gita. "When I say *juhi*, it is not generic jasmine, but again the fragrance in my mind conjures

a certain shape of flower which is unique."

Though growing up in different regions of India, Gita in the west and Pradip in the east, both Kars had childhoods filled with the sensual pleasures of nature and the garden. Gita remembers "an enchanted childhood," including Sunday visits to her beloved Aunt Banalata (which means "flower of the forest"), who "had such a green thumb. Her roses would be in bloom and it was so pretty all year round on her terrace garden."

Pradip can recall in loving detail trips to a relative's *bagan bari*, or garden house, outside the city. "On one side of the house would be these traditional Indian flowers with lovely fragrances, and on the other would be the orchard of mangoes, guavas, pineapple, and this divine fruit called *sitafal*. I think it's called custard apple [*Annona cherimola*] in English. There was a lawn

Pradip and his father, Rabindra Chandra, stand among the prized chrysanthemums. Photograph courtesy of Pradip Kar.

and an English garden. As kids we would go there, and the flowers would be in bloom and all this fruit was available. It was wonderful."

Pradip's father, Rabindra Chandra, was also an ardent gardener; he was a member of the Horticultural Society of Calcutta, a grower of prize-winning chrysanthemums, and an advice giver. "He was a very busy lawyer and didn't have a lot of time, but we always had a garden," explained Pradip. "His stenographers would come to work at six o'clock in the morning, and he would work for an hour. Then he'd stop at seven and have tea in the garden. There he'd have one or two people helping him, and he'd divide this plant and divide that. He grew the most beautiful chrysanthemums. That was his love."

After Gita and Pradip married and lived in the naval colony at New Delhi, they had space and time to garden seriously. "The garden was going to be the focal point of our energy," as Gita expressed it, "and the environment that our children would be brought up in. This was government property, and because of the transitory nature of service life, people didn't usually

invest too much in a big garden. But we decided that that was what we wanted to do."

"We didn't know much about gardening," she continued, "except about the indoor plants we'd had before. So we set about finding what would grow and what color and size each plant was and how to coordinate colors. We developed a kind of chart."

"In India the front of your house has the showy garden," said Pradip, "and the back has the vegetable patch. In our front garden we planned for sustained flowering through the whole growing period, from fall to spring. The summer months, when it's hot, are not a good time in the garden.

"We grew forty-two different kinds of annuals in addition to perennials. When the winter plants died back, we put in annuals we had grown from seed in the backyard—larkspur, calendula, marigolds, geraniums, cineraria, and double petunias, which were really difficult to grow. Our annual asters were lovely, with large flowers, and we had hollyhocks eight to ten feet high.

"Our younger daughter raised pansies. She wouldn't let anyone else

Just like in their Delhi garden, the Kars' Minnesota borders provide bloom throughout the season. In early summer, astilbe adds pastel tones and interesting textures to the beds.

grow those. They were her flower, and she had some in pots and some in the yard. When she was only ten years old, she won a prize for them at the Delhi Flower Show. Our older daughter provided us with much needed praise and adoration.

"Against the house, we had two plants of *madhu malti*, or honeycreeper. These were vines that used

to climb up the sides of the balcony. They were old plants. I don't really know how old they were. But typically when it was getting dark, we'd sit out on the lawn and look at them. The buds would open white and then slowly turn pink. From pink they would go to bright red magenta. The whole plant would be covered in blossoms, and the house would be heady with fragrance."

"When you came into our yard," added Gita, "there were these two silver oak trees and then the gardens, bounded by a henna hedge. As you entered, you got the feeling you were slipping into a different world."

Their garden was the showpiece of the colony. When their part-time gardener, Rameshwar, looked for work at other homes, he needed only to report that he worked at number 17. "Oh, the gardener at number 17," they would say in recognition of the Kars' lovely landscape.

The Kars are quick to credit others for their garden's success.

The clematis plants that climb the Kars' wooden fence are a tie with the many blooming vines of India.

The Kars enjoy the bright scarlet of lupine among the paler colors.

Rameshwar was a "wonderful gardener," said Gita. "He was a very poor man, and though he couldn't write about it, he knew a lot about gardening."

Pradip's father also was a big influence in the garden. "He brought a wealth of knowledge to us," Gita said. "He loved flowers and he loved trees. Every time he visited us, he brought seedlings."

"And he brought us a lot of advice," remembered Pradip, "how to grow various plants, the definition of 'sandy loam.' We had wonderful roses because he taught us how to prepare the soil and provide for adequate drainage.

"He got us to make our own fertilizer out of cow chips and the vegetable matter left from processing mustard-seed oil. It's terrible smelling," laughed Pradip, "but we called it the holy mixture because it was so good for the flowers."

"You could always know when the holy mixture was being administered," added Gita, "and people would say, 'What is that smell?' But we would pretend not to know and say, 'Oh, yes, what *is* that awful smell?'"

"He taught us how to pinch off buds," she continued, "so we would get the best blooms. But I always hated to do that. I wanted to have all the blossoms. So I would sneak a few pots off to the back so they would escape his eye."

Just as the Kars had planned, their garden became the center of family life. "All our work was a collaboration between my husband and me," said Gita. "It was a family affair. Everybody enjoyed it. Every Sunday I would cook up a big one-dish meal in the morning, and we would keep open house for our relatives and friends. Whoever dropped in would sit in the garden, and we would eat and have a cool drink together. There was a warm and friendly ambience."

From that experience the Kars emigrated to Minnesota in the early 1980s. "We loved gardening and wanted to do something in the yard," said Gita. "But in the first year we realized that it's a short growing season here. My husband had been so fond of roses, so he put in a few. The next year he planted a vegetable patch in the back."

"We grew the vegetables that we knew from India," said Pradip. "Tomatoes, of course, and eggplant and bush beans. We had a lot of success and that encouraged us."

They accumulated an indoor collection of tropical plants for their sunroom. "We have frangipani," said Gita. "It is our plant of hope. Also we grow white ginger, a flower with a beautiful blossom. We grow hibiscus, which we use in worship, and sweet basil, a sacred plant, and several varieties of jasmine. Pradip and I enjoy searching for new tropical plants together."

Soon the Kars realized that all their vegetables matured just when it was easy to buy them at the farmers' markets. So in the fourth year they gave up the vegetable patch and put in a patio and a large flower bed. As in India, they had to research what plants would grow, how tall they got, and how to coordinate colors. Once again they drew up a chart of flowers.

Echoing his comments about the Delhi garden, Pradip explained, "We planned for color and bloom throughout the season. Mostly we planted perennials, primrose, phlox, lupine, iris, daylily, Chinese rose, clematis, and astilbe. But also we used some annuals that we grew in India—marigolds, geraniums, larkspur, gerbera. In the front we put in a shade garden."

With this garden, the Kars began to feel at home in Coon Rapids.

"Culture is rooted in the land," Gita explained. "When you are not in the land of your culture, where do you grow your roots? I think we began to grow our roots into our American reality with the permanence of our garden and the trees we planted and the changing of the seasons."

They found that many of their satisfactions remained. "It is a great pleasure to work in the garden with the man who is my friend and partner," said Gita. "Pradip is from Bengal, and he knows a great deal of poetry of the seasons and the songs that celebrate them."

Added Pradip, "It is the most relaxing thing you can do, to just potter in the garden, tending the plants, digging them out, trimming off dead branches. You suddenly stop concentrating on other things and are in the here and now and in contact with the earth. That is what life is all about."

JASMINE
(Jasminaceae)

he jasmine, or jessamine, belongs botanically to *Jasminum* and contains about 150 species, mostly natives of the warmer regions of Asia. Many jasmines are vines or shrubs with highly fragrant flowers. The white jasmine (*Jasminum grandiflorum*) is the plant highly prized by perfumers for its large flowers and heavy fragrance. The blossoms open every morning and are gathered after sunrise because the dew will injure their fragrance. One acre of land yields about five hundred pounds of bloom. For many years, the delicate, sweet odor of *J. grandiflorum* could not be produced artificially. Now a close synthetic, Otto of Jasmine, exists, but the true fragrance is not exactly reproducible.

The Zambak, or Arabian jasmine (*J. sambac*) is an evergreen white-flowered climber valued for its scent. Hindus string the flowers together as neck garlands for honored guests and use the blossoms as offerings in religious ceremonies. At Ghazipur, a town on the Ganges, jasmine, called *Chameli* there, is used for making perfumed oils. In China *Jasminum paniculatum* is grown for scenting tea.

Chue Yang

LONG BEANS AND LEMONGRASS

s a young girl in Laos, Chue Yang rode water buffalo and horses and worked in her family's fields of corn, rice, greens, and herbs. Today she drives a car to her white-collar job in Minneapolis. Like many immigrants, Chue is a woman with ties to two cultures. When questioned, she will attest to the difficulties of adjusting: "We struggle so much." But she will also modestly acknowledge that she's succeeding ably: "We have very good children," and "I have been promoted four different times."

Chue is a thoroughly modern wife and mother with a full-time job and a house in the suburbs. At the same time she works to maintain many of her Hmong traditions for herself and her family. After all, Chue was twenty-two years old when she, her husband, Her, and their eight-month-old daughter left Laos sixteen years ago.

Her growing-up years were spent on the family farm and in the vil-

lage. She helped tend the animals—eight horses, thirty water buffalo, sixty cows, and more than a hundred pigs—and remembers working in the fields from the age of four.

"Back home we have so much," she recalled. "We planted four acres of rice, ten acres of corn, banana trees, and pineapples. My mom is a person who likes to have everything and doesn't like to ask for things. So we grew potatoes and sweet potatoes, four kinds of mustard greens. We had soybeans, two kinds of sugarcane, squash, and Chinese eggplant, which has a small fruit and tender skin. My mom had an herbal garden that was almost as big as my lawn is today. [Chue's suburban lawn is about one hundred feet square.] We had ginger and plants with no American names. One called *piocha* grows underground and you eat the roots."

In Laos, the farmers use swidden (slash-and-burn) techniques to pre-

pare the fields. When one area becomes fallow, the family will prepare other land. Over time, cultivated fields may be some distance from the village. Still, the whole family, several generations, walks each day to tend the crops. "Over there we have no machines to help," explained Chue. "You do it all by your hand. You just carry everything on your back."

The work was hard, but it helped make Yang a strong, resourceful person. She came here in 1981 and

As she did in Laos, Chue maintains a huge vegetable garden. Not laid out in rows, the patches of squash, corn, and beans grow together through the summer.

"didn't know a single English word. For the first two years, my husband and I got lost everywhere," she said with a laugh. By 1988, she was a translator for the St. Paul-Ramsey Medical Center. "It was a good job," she said, "but it made me sad to see people sick, and there was no chance for promotion." Chue quickly found employment that offered better opportunities. When their inner-city neighborhood in Minneapolis became too risky for their children ("we had to wait at the bus stop with our girls," she said), the Yangs bought a house in Brooklyn Park.

In many ways, Chue and Her are living out the American dream, but they want to keep their Hmong culture alive for their six children. The family speaks Hmong with each other and participates in Southeast Asian festivals. "I tell them about a lot of things in Laos," she said, "and they listen politely, but I think they don't keep our culture."

The Yangs' gardens are the most visible reminder of their heritage. Chue would garden because she loves it so much, if for no other reason. "It wakes me up to go to my plants," she enthused. "I may be tired in the morning, but as soon as I go out and look at what's growing, it lifts me up."

But in keeping her gardens, Yang is keeping her culture. After all, in Laos her whole life was spent in the fields, broadcasting seeds or hoeing for weeds, harvesting mustard greens or drying onion sets for the year ahead. Here, she uses many of the same methods and raises the same crops. By observing Chue's Minnesota plots, her children get a sense of life back in Laos.

Chue's gardens are no small commitment, and a challenge to people who maintain they have no time to raise vegetables. In her backyard plot (forty-five by twenty feet), she grows cucumbers (including a dark, round variety), eggplants, green and chile peppers, multiplier onions *(Allium cepa,* variety *aggregatum),* bush and long *(Vigna unguiculata,* variety *sesquipedalis)* beans, several kinds of mustard greens, and winter squash (including a long, green

LEMONGRASS
(Cymbopogon citratus)

ost likely originating in tropical Asia, lemongrass is unknown in the wild, but is widely cultivated in the tropics for its aromatic oil. Tapered, three-foot long leaves form a dense clump of green. When crushed or cut, they emit a strong lemon fragrance. The oil is used in perfumery, medicine, and for flavoring. The Latin name comes from the Greek word for boat, *kymbe*, and for beard, *pogon*.

Lemongrass. Photograph by David Cavagnaro.

variety big enough to "feed Minneapolis," according to Chue). Lemongrass *(Cymbopogon citratus)*, cilantro, dill, mint, and basil are but a few of her culinary herbs. Medicinal herbs, like "duck-foot herb" and "chicken medicine" (species unknown), seen as beneficial for numerous conditions, are two of the many she grows. To improve the soil's fertility, Chue throws all her vegetable wastes on the plot; her husband digs in fermented grass clippings.

Indoors, Yang grows hibiscus, "which grew outside the door in Laos," she said, and numerous medicinal plants. She cultivates spider plant *(Chlorophytum comosum)* for a sore throat ("back home we rub it on"), green philodendron for tonsillitis, and purple philodendron to ease a sore throat. "Beefsteak plant" *(Perilla frutescens)* works for burns. The ubiquitous "chicken medicine" plant is on hand as a potion for new mothers. "One day I would like to have a greenhouse to grow all this," she said. "An herb garden is important for a Hmong family."

The biggest plot lies ten minutes away in Coon Rapids. Yang, like many other Hmong, rents acreage from a local farmer to grow the crops that will not fit in her backyard plot. There, she and her mother have one acre of land planted in huge patches of winter squash, cucumbers, melons, amaranth, beans ("Asians love pole beans more than anything," she said), mustard greens, sugar snap peas, and multiplier onions. Along the edges they have planted corn and sugarcane.

Simply naming the plants can hardly do justice to the complexity of Chue's garden. The cucumbers, for example, are of several varieties. Chue called attention to a "white" cucumber with yellow flesh, a "French" one with a red interior, and pickling varieties. There are at least five types of mustard greens, which differ in leaf shape and culinary use. One is prized for its flower stalk, others for their leaves. The "Thai," is "very nice," according to Chue. There are two plants from the solanum family. One called *ong choy* is eaten like spinach. Chue and her mother harvest not only the fruit, but the stem and blossom ends of the squash and pea plants.

One of the Yangs' favorite vegetables is the long bean, seen here growing up a simple support.

At this plot, Chue and the others cultivate vegetables much as they might have done in Laos. They use no fertilizer or watering system, family members help with planting and harvesting, and seeds are collected and saved each year. When planting, Chue and her mother do not dig; in fact, there are no digging tools in Laos. Instead, they rough up the ground with a short-handled hoe, then broadcast seed.

There are no beds or rows here, no paths or walkways; rather, big patches of vegetables crowd against each other. When the fields become weedy or less productive, they will be abandoned, mirroring the rhythm of swidden techniques.

On weekends, as families gather at the plots, the garden becomes the center of social life, just as it was in Laos. "We don't just garden here," Chue explained. "Our husbands barbecue, the cousins play, and we do a lot of visiting."

The gardens supply hundreds of pounds of produce during the season, keeping the Yangs and their extended family well fed. Chue and her sisters freeze corn, greens, and cucumbers for winter use. Many plants are left in the ground to go to seed for the next year. In addition, Chue gives away "so much—to my friends, to coworkers. When my mother runs out of vegetables, she doesn't go to the store, she goes to the garden."

Chue is somewhat surprised by her own interest in gardening. "When I was little, I had to help my mother with her herbs, but I couldn't step on anything. I used to say, 'In my life I will never do that.' Now I like it and I say, 'Don't walk on my garden.' I'm a person who likes to be outside. When I get home from work, even before I go in, I come out here and see how things are doing."

usan Davis Price, a resident of St. Paul, has lived and gardened in Minnesota for over twenty years. She lectures frequently on the history of Minnesota gardens and writes for home and garden publications, including *Minnesota Horticulturist*, *Urban Forests*, *Victorian Homes*, and *American Gardener*. Her first book, *Minnesota Gardens: An Illustrated History*, won the Quill and Trowel Award from the Garden Writers' Association of America, as well as a Minnesota Book Award.

ohn Gregor, owner of ColdSnap Photography, specializes in garden and nature photography and is a regular contributor to *Minnesota Monthly*, *Midwest Home and Garden*, and *The Minnesota Conservation Volunteer*. He lives in Minneapolis.